INSCAPE 2019

Washburn University

Department of English

1700 SW College Ave

Topeka, KS 66621

While with an eye made quiet by the power
Of harmony, and the deep power of joy,
We see into the life of things.

–William Wordsworth

Vol. 44

inscapemagazine.org
washburn.edu/inscape
facebook.com/inscapemagazine

Cover Art:
Detail from *Black Hole in the Milky Way*
Tanya Shatseva
acrylic on canvas
12x12

Inscape, published by the English Department at Washburn University in Topeka, Kansas, features poetry, fiction, nonfiction, and visual art from the region and beyond.

GLORIOUS

Jack Granath

I

used

to

be

a

glorious

tree.

Some

ed-

i-

tor

did

this

to

me.

INSCAPE 2019

EDITORS IN CHIEF

Madi Weidenbach
Jack Williamson

FICTION EDITORS

Stephanie Teater (Section Co-Chief)
Sydney Van Dyke (Section Co-Chief)
Joshua Maler
Alex Ruecker
Taylor Schiefelbein

POETRY EDITORS

Anna Ciummo (Section Chief)
Halle Cybulski
Sarah Stickley
Lierin Woods

NONFICTION EDITORS

Adam White (Section Chief)
Zachariah King
Madi Weidenbach
Jack Williamson

ART EDITORS

Lierin Woods (Section Chief)
Anna Ciummo
Joshua Maler
Taylor Schiefelbein

MAGAZINE DESIGN

Timothy Christopher Ryan Volpert

FACULTY ADVISOR

Eric McHenry

POETRY

ART

FICTION

NONFICTION

HYBRID

Editors'
Choice

Io Sono Un Sogno
Charly Verger
oil on canvas
35.5x35.5

REBIRTH
Charly Verger
oil on canvas
45.6x35

Heartless

Teresa Milbrodt

It was easier to sleep with my heart outside my body, resting on the nightstand. I told my wife it was so I didn't have nightmares, and while I worried she'd think I was a sissy, she nodded and didn't comment. She knew I fretted about everything—finances, home repairs, people at the assisted living facility where I worked—so I guess it made sense.

I made up the lie about nightmares because if I'd told my wife that she was the reason for sleeping without my heart, she wouldn't have cared, and that would have been worse. Still, I didn't expect to wake up one morning and discover my heart was missing. I couldn't find it under the bed or behind the nightstand. My wife was not sympathetic.

"It was a matter of time before something like this happened," she said at breakfast. She always made the coffee and I told her how much I appreciated that. "You lose things all the time. I bet it's beside the bed under your dirty underwear. Or maybe the cat knocked it off. You'll find it again."

I drank my coffee and was surprised I didn't need sugar like usual. I wasn't sick or sore, just a little empty, but more than that I had a detached sense of worry. What if my heart had fallen into the wrong hands? What if someone had come into our house in the middle of the night and stolen it? My wife told me not to be silly, since there were no signs of breaking and entering.

I said, "There doesn't have to be breaking, just entering."

"You're being dramatic," she said, implying my heart wasn't that important. "Eat your toast and look for it later, when you have a clear head."

But my head was clear and my heart was not under the dirty underwear. My wife's heart stayed in her chest, so she didn't have to worry about these things.

"My job gives me enough worry," she said. She was a pediatric nurse, so I knew those words were true.

After eating her toast, my wife left for work. I finished my coffee and stared out the window. For a moment I wondered what I should do, but I picked up my car keys from the table and drove to the assisted living facility. That was the most dutiful course of action, and when you don't have a heart, perhaps it's easier to concentrate on duty.

I'd been sleeping without my heart in my chest for three years, maybe longer, since my wife stopped kissing me in the morning and before bed. I didn't know what else to do. What was the correct course of action when you loved someone, yet had a feeling that they were settling for you? I didn't understand the transition, how we started out in love and ended up as co-owners of the same house who happened to share a bed. The best thing I could say about my marriage was that it was mostly polite.

My wife was resigned to the partnership like it was a car she'd bought and didn't like but didn't want to sell. She didn't seem to care that I loved her dearly, or rather loved the person she'd been, who was intelligent and funny and cuddly and thoughtful. Now she was tired, and quiet, but bodies at rest tend to stay at rest when they have gainful employment, a mortgage, and two car loans.

Usually I put my heart in before I went to work because I needed to be delicate there, delicate and caring since I worked around elderly people and stressed-out nurses and stressed-out family members though I was in the finance department. I ordered supplies for the facility and paid bills and sometimes acted as on-demand muscle when someone called me from the hall to help a patient who needed assistance getting into or out of a wheelchair.

Most of the residents had meals in the dining room. I had lunch with them, and sometimes dinner, since my wife didn't care about eating together and said she'd have a can of soup or a peanut butter sandwich. She ate a big lunch in the hospital cafeteria where she and the other nurses conferenced about their small patients. That world was intimately hers, and one I did not want to enter.

"Those folks at the assisted living facility need company," she told me, meaning she did not need company, at least not my company. Thinking about that was hurtful on the days when I had my heart in, but now that it had been lost, I was okay. I worked on budgets and spreadsheets, gave my assistant Amanda a couple inventory tasks, and wondered if someone was trying to do something evil with my heart, like enchant it to make me devoid of a soul. Or perhaps they were gluing lace and sequins to it, or cooking it with rice to make soup.

I was not excited for lasagna at lunch, and wondered if I should have taken a sick day, or a heartsick day, but that would be more trouble to explain than it was worth. Part of coming to work without my heart wasn't bad. Everything struck me as a cool breeze, passing information about the number of cans of tomatoes and beans we needed to order, and the bottles of ibuprofen we had in the medications closet, and that Helen needed a hand getting into her wheelchair for a doctor's appointment. I wasn't cold, or unhelpful. I gave people hugs. I smiled.

When I sat down at my desk after lunch, I wondered where my heart had gone, and in the same absent sentence reflected on how suggesting divorce to my wife wouldn't be worth it. She'd look at me and say, "Why would we do that?" ending the discussion. We didn't have kids but I thought we needed a crisis to split, something to tell people so separation would seem legitimate. But neither of us felt like having an affair or racking up a ridiculous amount of credit card debt. Telling people my marriage had fizzled out would result in a lot of shrugs, and co-workers saying, "Yeah, so much for romance. Welcome to married life."

I'd heard someone say that you should have at least three marriages, even if they're to the same person. When you look at it that way you can't avoid having three marriages, probably more, and it makes sense that you would like some of them more than others, but if you hit upon one that you didn't like, what were you supposed to do? Wait for the next phase?

For the first several years of our marriage my wife had asked how my day went, but I didn't ask how her day went because then she'd tell me. I thought sometimes she should take her heart out, too, since it would have helped her to be less stressed. She brought the shadows of her child patients home from the hospital. I saw them standing around our kitchen table, looking like they wanted to ask for a cookie or a hug. It was difficult for nurses to find the right-sized heart, not too big and not too small. Maybe they couldn't fit everyone inside their hearts all the time. I shouldn't have been surprised. Or upset. And I wasn't upset, since my heart was still missing.

After work I didn't feel like going home. I knew I needed to find my damn heart, which didn't explain why I ended up sitting alone at a restaurant with a beer and a plate of cheddar bacon potato skins with sour cream, something my wife would have told me would lead to a heart attack. Could my heart be attacked if I couldn't find it? Maybe it was currently under attack, so it didn't matter if I ate the potato skins since the whole thing was out of my hands.

When we were first dating, my wife would have eaten potato skins, but now she worried about her hips and cholesterol, though I told her that both of those things were fine. Too often I found myself wishing she were more like the person I'd dated, the person I'd married. I still thought she was beautiful, but she didn't smile anymore, she didn't joke. I couldn't lie and say that I'd been the same person for twenty-three years, but I kept hoping my old wife would come back. The new wife still knew who I was and retained her old memories, which was more disturbing than if those thoughts had been lost in the transition to her new identity.

I ordered another beer and wondered what to do about my lost heart, if I should hire a private investigator or scour the whole house or forget about it and focus on my job. Today after lunch when one of the nurses told me that Pearl, a longtime resident, would need to go to a nursing home, I didn't cry. I comforted the nurse instead, because she was crying, and it struck me how many different occasions there were in which it would be nice to have my heart outside my body forever, such as funerals and budget meetings. Objectivity could be an asset.

As I drank my beer I started hoping that my heart stayed lost. Maybe when I returned home, I'd find evidence of an intrusion around my nightstand or bedroom door, a bit of hair from an ogre, shimmering green snake scales, or a thread of silver witch's hair that disappeared in a puff of smoke. It would be nice to have an excuse to take a few days off work, get in the car, and go on a quest. I had plenty of vacation time, and my assistant Amanda was a sharp young woman with an accounting degree, a nice boyfriend, and a great heart. She could handle the office on her own for a week or two.

When I got home my wife was watching TV and gave me a nod from the living room.

I resumed the search for my heart with a new sense of purpose, scouring the floor around our window, the hallway outside our bedroom door, and the carpet around my nightstand, poking my fingers into small corners and hoping to find a speck of magic.

Instead I found my heart. It had wedged in the tiny space under my nightstand, which had short legs that lifted it an inch off the floor. I hadn't thought my heart could fit there, but it was wide and thin and must have slid a little on the carpet. I couldn't get it with my thick fingers, so I had to pull the nightstand out from the wall. I sat on the floor for a moment with my lint-covered heart, listening to the TV. Then I stood up and tucked my heart in my pocket and walked into the living room. I knew I needed to say something, ask difficult questions while my heart was still out of my body.

"How was your day?" I said. My wife was still slumped on the couch.

"Okay," she said in a low tone that made it clear the opposite was true. "I'm tired."

“Would you like some tea?” I asked. “Is there anything you want to talk about?”

“Why?” she said. When she turned to me her eyes were hard, almost accusatory.

“No reason,” I said. “I still can’t find my heart.”

“Too bad,” she said, looking back at the set. “Maybe tomorrow.”

I returned to our bedroom and sat on the edge of the bed, reading a magazine article on how vitamins weren’t that great for you, at least in pill form. After a few minutes, my wife turned off the TV and walked past me to the bathroom to get ready for bed. She came out wearing her cotton nightgown, put on her sleep mask, and tucked herself under the covers, facing the window. I slipped into the bathroom, took my heart out of my pocket, and washed off the lint and dust. I dried my heart on a washcloth, then padded to the living room to watch TV and make microwave popcorn, which was another thing my wife swore would kill me. In those dark moments without my heart, I wondered why she cared.

After finishing the popcorn, I figured my heart and I could take a drive on I-80, and head west with the big rigs. I wasn’t tired, and around five in the morning we could stop at a diner in Illinois, eat a greasy breakfast, watch the sun come up, and see how we felt. I slid my heart in my pocket. It was a durable little thing, I knew that now, but I felt it beating while I was in the kitchen looking for my car keys. The pulse was slight and insistent. It wanted to be back in my chest.

I removed my heart from my pocket, clean and pink and weary of being in the cold world. I closed my eyes, cool metal keys in one hand and heart in the other, then I slid the keys in my pocket, my heart in my chest, and crept to the bedroom. My wife was breathing heavily, the deep inhalations of slumber. Gently, so gently, I reached into her chest and cradled her heart in my palm. She’d be mad if she woke up, but I removed it so carefully she didn’t stir.

I worried her heart would be encased in stone, but no, it was huge and delicate with thin gold walls, a heart three times the size of mine, and soft to the touch. Her heart was tarnished, patchworked, and etched with too many names. My name was there, along with the names of many people I didn't know. Her patients. This was a heart that held hundreds. There wasn't room for any more, but I knew she would find space because she had to. Her heart beat slowly in my hand, each pulse a blush of pink light. I washed my wife's heart in the bathroom sink, using warm water and rose-scented soap, then I buffed it to a dull shine with a washcloth and slipped her heart back in her chest, knowing it would tarnish again.

I sat beside her, on the edge of our bed. The car keys in my pocket jabbed my leg. My heart beat in my own chest, slow and steady and back home. I removed my shirt. I removed my pants. I dropped them into the darkness beside the bed and curled around my wife, cupping her body in mine, my hand over her beating heart, feeling the texture of those names through her skin, feeling my own heart try to match the pulse of hers.

Four Months, One Week

Laurie Reiche

Four months, one week
since you made me young.
The honeysuckle is blossoming.
Four months, one week
since what was meant to be had begun.
Morning clouds are cold; the house is warm.
We are the oldest newness,
love conceived out of wedlock.
What do we do now with the miracle?
I've made a little garden
and will watch the flowers grow.

Editors' Choice

Election Night Clinic

JoDean Nicolette

My medical assistant doesn't usually swear at work. And at first I didn't notice, as I stepped out of exam room nine, the door clicking quietly behind me. I was perplexed, ruminating on how to help Mrs. Gonzalez, who waited in a flimsy paper gown on the exam table. I looped my stethoscope around my neck, oblivious not only to my medical assistant Rosa as she cursed at whatever was on her computer screen, but also to the custodian pushing his rattling cart. I knocked into him, toppling his mop over, sloshing water across the floor. Flustered, I apologized and bent to help, but he smiled and waved me off as he soaked up the puddle and vanished around the corner.

In my own defense, I hardly expect to encounter anyone in the hallway on Tuesday nights. Usually it's just Rosa and I, under the fluorescents, the world dark and invisible outside the windows. Rosa leads the patients from the waiting room to their appointments, and then back out, one at a time. We know there are other people in the building, like the custodian and the triage nurse, but we encounter only a suggestion of their presence: an empty trash bin, a whistle heard from around the corner, or a new name with an urgent complaint tucked stealthily into the schedule. It's one of the reasons we like Tuesday nights. Unlike the constant buzz and bustle of the day shift, evening clinic is unpopulated, the quiet broken only by the low hum of the refrigerators and the occasional squeak of shoes on the linoleum.

"Shit!" Rosa spit out, pecking at the screen with her lacquered nail. Knocked into awareness by a mop and bucket, I registered Rosa's voice, and leaned in to look.

"What?" I asked, thinking the triage nurse had added another patient after an already hectic evening. This Tuesday had been busy: blood pressure checks, lupus, diabetes, a twisted knee, a twisted ankle, asthma. I had been surprised, because it was election night. Rosa and I had assumed that people would be home following the results.

"Blue! No, those states need to be blue!" Rosa threw up her hands. She looked at me, "This isn't happening."

***

No, it's not, I thought. *It can't be.* I dismissed my apprehension, shook my head, forced myself to focus again on Mrs. Gonzalez. She was here because of her back, and I didn't know what to do. I know how to manage back pain—that's bread and butter for a primary care physician. It's that Mrs. Gonzalez was undocumented, so although she worked long days—back-breaking days—as a cleaning woman, she had no health insurance. She would have to pay outright for what she might need: medications, imaging, physical therapy. And because she worked without any other benefits, she also couldn't afford what she required most, which was time to rest and recover. My clinic, which is a federally qualified health center (FQHC), specializes in care for publicly funded patients, like those with Medicaid (Medi-Cal in California), Medicare, or our county plan. These patients can get most of what they need, including doctor visits, medications, and ancillary services. Completely unfunded patients, like Mrs. Gonzalez, receive doctor visits on a sliding scale, and some labs and medications at low cost, but other services like X-rays or other imaging, diagnostic tests, specialists, or physical therapy would be cash-pay, and expensive—prohibitively so, on her minimum-wage salary.

"I don't like to bother *la doctora,*" Mrs. Gonzalez had said, "but the pain is very bad, and I must be able to work." For the last six months she had been working, and living, with the pain. At first, she had assumed it was a small pain, the type she might expect as a *señora de la limpieza*, and that it would self-resolve. Then, after a few weeks, she'd tried medications from *la tienda,* and even researched back exercises on her *amiga's* computer. She relayed the scene for me, the stretches and contortions on the linoleum in her kitchen, her nieces and nephews giggling and snorting at her positions, her grunts, and her groans. Mrs. Gonzalez finally came into the clinic when nothing helped and the ache became too much, interfering with both her work and her rest.

"I know, *Doctora*," she said, nodding, "that you can make me feel better."

Before I could stop myself, I sighed out loud and collapsed a little on my stool. I hated being put on a pedestal; it made me feel like an imposter. Her needs were so many, and without insurance there was so little I could do to help. Mrs. Gonzalez looked alarmed, as if she had done something wrong. "I'm sorry," I told her, flushing and closing my eyes. "It's not you. *Un momento*, let me check on what resources we have for you."

I faced the familiar tangle of thoughts and feelings that accompanied visits like this. First I tamped down the guilt—at being born to a middle-class family in America, at being white, at taking wealth and education for granted. I had gone to Stanford Medical School, something I'd always thought I would be proud of. But instead, when people inquired, I often avoided the question, or said it under my breath. Or blushed. The name felt like a badge, a tiara, a label that screamed out privilege… an arrow pointing at me, *This one had a leg up!* I also took health insurance for granted, never contemplating anything but complete access to who and what I needed. And now, as a physician, I had the healthcare red carpet: back-line numbers, immediate callbacks, or "curbsides" passing in the halls, waived fees and free medications. The last time I had had back pain, a colleague ushered me into an empty exam room between patients and performed a curative osteopathic maneuver. Within minutes my pain had vanished and I continued with my work day, forgetting about the incident altogether.

But the facts of the situation were different for Mrs. Gonzalez. Like a million other Californians, she had entered this country outside the formal immigration process, so she had minimal access to services. Some people in this situation, I can help in a small way. They have simple needs like an acute laceration requiring stitches or an infection I can treat. Or blood-pressure management that responds to an inexpensive medication we carry in our little pharmacy. But others, like Mrs. Gonzalez, have conditions that need more than our system can provide. Physical therapy, for example, or an X-ray or MRI. Or most importantly, time. She needed time to rest and recover. But she had no access to sick time, vacation time, or workers' compensation for an injury sustained on the job. And if she took days off, the loss of income might push her and her family off the razor-sharp edge of survival, if she didn't lose her job altogether.

On most nights, I am up for the challenge; I brainstorm with Rosa to find services, make extra phone calls to unearth county resources, and call in favors. But after such a long night my guard was down, and I felt a familiar stab of frustration and resentment. First, I directed too much of my frustration at Mrs. Gonzalez and her expectations. Her unrealistic trust that I could make her feel better—simply solve the problem—felt unfair. *Do I have a magic wand?* I griped to myself. I *mean, she snuck in here, into this country and into a system that doesn't support her. She signed up for this impossible life, and now she's in here expecting me to fix it.* I had no option but to fail; I was a failure. I couldn't give her the things that might really help her.

But of course none of this was Mrs. Gonzalez's fault. I redirected my self-absorption to ire at the real problem: our health-care system. I had gone to medical school to help people, all people. I am a physician who believes that health care is a basic human right, not a privilege. Not only for people like me. Not subject to what language you speak, or what card you carry in your wallet, or how much money you have, or behind which arbitrary boundary you were born. Instead, I am working in a system that is fragmented and lopsided, listing heavily toward those with financial resources. The system stacks itself against people like Mrs. Gonzalez, the working poor, regardless of their citizenship. Where I live, in northern California's wine country, the residents have built their wealth on the backs of farm workers, documented and not. Was this the best we could offer them? I'd faced many similar scenarios in the last fifteen years, mostly citizens who were working poor, making too much to qualify for assistance programs, but too little to afford the exorbitant costs of health insurance. Patients who came to the doctor because their symptoms had become debilitating or frightening, but who could not afford the studies or treatments they needed. Mr. Roberts, for example, barely able to rise in the morning with his ankylosing spondylitis, but who couldn't afford the X-rays or expensive treatments. Or Mrs.

Marley, who had chest pain but wouldn't undergo any heart testing. Or Ms. Rhodes, who came in for weight loss, new headaches, and double-vision. Her symptoms were suspicious for widely spread cancer, and I wasn't surprised to find a mass in her right breast. She'd never had a mammogram or other preventive care because she couldn't afford it. Despite my urging, she refused to go to the ER treatment, dreading the five-figure bill that would arrive in the mail. Remembering Ms. Rhodes, I felt embarrassed. I had harangued her. "Look, I can't help you here in the clinic; it's too serious. Your expectations are unrealistic; you have to go to the emergency room. Just go! Lots of people don't pay, it's your life we're talking about here." But she shook her head, and I knew we were thinking of the same horror stories, of people going bankrupt and losing their homes. Stories that I knew seemed more real to Ms. Rhodes than to me.

I thought back to the year before when I'd had a breast mass evaluated. I took the necessary time off work, and the system made it happen, quickly and conveniently. The initial imaging, the second look, the biopsy, the specialist consultation, all within a week. I received my results immediately in a cell phone call. When it was all over, my insurance hadn't covered about $1,000 of the enormous bill, so I wrote a check and it all flew out of my mind. But for Ms. Rhodes, who had to ask a week in advance to get a half day off, without pay, to discuss her severe symptoms with a doctor, the whole system seemed like a Goliath. After she left, I was haunted for the rest of the day with the image of her dying alone at home, sprawled on her shag carpet after a stroke or a blood clot, or after one of the tumors that likely grew in her brain got so big it was incompatible with further consciousness. Sometimes the temptation nagged at me, to flee this clinic—the relentless flow of people who needed more than what we could offer—and settle into a nice boutique practice, or an HMO. As if averting my eyes would make this problem go away.

Still, in the last few years, my job has gotten easier. I remembered another evening in November, in 2009, standing behind my husband Ben, our eyes riveted on the TV. On CNN. Ben held my hands as I rested them on his shoulders. Neither of us dared make a sound, as if our voices could disrupt the tide of change in our legislature. The House of Representatives was casting their ballots on Barack Obama's Affordable Care Act. I squeezed Ben's hands with each "yes" vote as the numbers flashed on the screen: 211, 212...tears filled my eyes…213, 214, 215, 216, 217…218! Ben and I jumped up together, our hands raised in the air. An American healthcare plan! My chest swelled and I shook with excitement. I couldn't remember a time I had felt so proud of my president and my country.

I read the statistics that thirty million Americans would receive new access to medical services, but even as a physician, that statistic didn't mean much to me outside of a flutter in my chest. The real relief came in what I saw on a day-to-day level, the number of patients eligible for Medi-Cal doubled, and the working poor could afford health insurance. At work we wore buttons on our white coats that said, *Ask me about covered California*, our state-based website for selecting a plan. Our staff helped patients surf the exchanges, and we received additional funding to serve the increased number of people who presented themselves to see a doctor. Before that day in 2009, I dreaded asking the question, "Do you have insurance?" First, because I despised the system that required it, and I couldn't stand the idea that my patients might think it made a difference to me. But with such wide treatment disparities based on finances, I had to know, to create a realistic plan for the patient. Second, I hated the question because the answer was so often, "No." Or a red-faced, awkward silence, because the patient was afraid their answer would reveal their documentation status. I ached with disappointment each time. But now, with the Affordable Care Act, it was easier to ask because I knew that many patients could, would nod, and I would feel empowered to help. Even patients like Mrs. Gonzalez, who still had no funding, would benefit because our clinic could offer sliding scale services like osteopathic manipulation, acupuncture, and massage.

***

These services—the things I *could* offer Mrs. Gonzales—are what claimed my attention when I stepped out into the hallway, crashing into the custodian and hearing my medical assistant's distress at the election results. I rested my elbows on the counter next to Rosa's work station, fingers on my forehead, massaging my temples. We watched the map of the United States on the computer screen. The states that had been light blue—*leaning blue*—had turned pink. Florida, Pennsylvania, Ohio. I felt powerless. And I felt angry. I glared at Florida and Pennsylvania, caricatures of voters flashing through my head: hunched, obese, wheezing men and women waiting in line at the polls in the Northeast. Over-tanned and wrinkled in the South, with cigarettes hanging from their lips. The same unhealthy people who destroyed their own bodies were infecting the rest of us with their self-destruction. *Those people.* I shook my head again, ashamed. I have a "big" self and a "little" self, and this self-absorbed, bitter person dominating my clinic tonight was definitely my little self. When I see patients, I need compassion and generosity. Rapping the bell of my stethoscope on the counter, and taking a moment to breathe, I tried to shake free of the anger and the judgement.

"Don't tell me any more until I'm done with clinic," I said, grabbing the list of resources, a patient handout, and fleeing to see Mrs. Gonzalez. But even sequestered in the room, in a protected and private space that is supposed to house only me and my patient, I felt the evening's events crowding in. My phone buzzed in my pocket, and in a distracted, compulsive need to check for an emergency, I pulled it out and glanced down. The text was from my husband. *Are you following this disaster?* The words glowered at me from the tiny screen. They consumed me, invading the exam room, my concentration, this patient's life. Despite my efforts, my thoughts became murky, and the clinic surreal. Surely I would wake in a few hours to a beautiful sunrise… Mrs. Gonzalez would be pain free, and we would be celebrating yet another landmark in Washington, D.C. Because this couldn't be happening, right?

***

I struggled to complete the visit with Mrs. Gonzalez. Stepping out to allow her to dress, I was relieved to be finished—released from the struggle to concentrate. But I dreaded the anxiety and uncertainty that waited. In a few minutes, Rosa would knock on the door to exam room nine, and summarize my recommendations, and then accompany Mrs. Gonzalez to the front to check out. I knew the waiting room would be empty except for the plastic chairs, the abandoned magazines, and a few scattered toys. Rosa and I would finish up our documentation, shut down the computers, and then shuffle out the side door through the empty lot to our cars.

But this Tuesday night, the clinic was not empty. A group had gathered at Rosa's workstation. The custodian, the security guard, the triage nurse, and the receptionist had all emerged from their solitary posts and crowded around Rosa and her computer. The screen glowed like a campfire, and the clinic staff huddled around it, shoulders touching, silently drawn in by an ancient instinct to seek warmth and companionship to fend off the cold and the dark. I stood behind them, my hands in my pockets. None of us spoke as the electoral votes tilted more and more in favor of past tragedies. Tilting away from us, tilting toward those like me. The screen glowed redder and redder before our eyes, the country burning itself up. I couldn't fight off the despair anymore, the guilt, the horrible sensation of falling back into the abyss.

"Shit!" I said, shattering the stillness, just as Mrs. Gonzalez stuck her head out of exam room nine, to check on what was taking so long. When none of us broke away from the computer to assist her, she left alone, walking herself down the hallway and out into the night.

3 Men 2016 Mixed
Ira Joel Haber
mixed
9.5x7.5

Peaches

Maxima Kahn

This morning as i looked
into the gleaming
white plastic compost bucket—
three rotting peaches turned blue allover—
i thought of you
and all that's rotting,
all that gives fruit, lets fruit fall,
perishes, all that was once
golden, perfected,
offered itself freely
in the painted enamel bowl
until a blueness began to crawl,
hidden at first,
from the underbelly on up,
embracing, covering,
becoming peach, peach-mold, blue
peach, too tender, flesh falling,
so it's cast on the heap
where the fallen things, the rotten things,
what's spent or no longer needed,
the inedible portions,
wait in the placid harmony of the useless
to become new life again.

Listening in the Family Cemetery

Larry Thacker

> *"Ultimately, psychic automatism is a process such that its dynamics cannot be fully appreciated or understood from simply viewing the writing or the drawing that results."*
>
> A Boatload of Madmen —*Dickran Tashjian*

Every spare step a death notice to the vision, a noted surprise,
marbleized, engraved along unmoving stone like manuscripts
wanting read. Grass, sporadic weeds, off-shooting random prayers
star-ward in the day, asking only to be received, heard.
Like dance step instructions:
Brick, brass, marble. Breath.

The finely packed earth finally cooperates with the echo
of neatly stacked bodies, homes hollowed out of hallowed ground.
All seeming still. Nothing still.
The bob of branches, a turn of rain
informed leaves, that shift of two tones of green within every tree.
And then the messages, as the truck full of coal rumbles by:

We are tired of all the traffic
The lichens itch our long back of bark
We have never liked fake flowers
The man who comes to mow twice a month seems nice

The baby wild ferns shift in a gentled wind. Rest.

Everywhere is as always, a fading of plastic red to pink
and very slow lightening of silky green ribbon on wire stems.

Sophia Loren Making a Pizza

Benjamin Harnett

This is the kind of thing we post now,
in-between pleas for a restoration of sanity
and airline customer-service complaints,
in-between links to articles about celebrity beefs,
and articles about the slow-motion apocalypse
of global warming. An old colorized picture
of Sophia Loren, in Napoli, making a pizza.

"It's been a hard day; we deserve this."

I have to wade through GIFs to get to it,
a Japanese mascot running
from bombs, in another a large bear on a small
bench, in a pristine wilderness,
yawns. Sophia is not dressed for it.
A small can of tomato paste has two plump
tomatoes, pressed together like breasts.

"These are upsetting times, folks. So—"

A dish of anchovies. A glass bottle of olive oil
the colorist should have tinted green
and not brown. She swirls sauce onto
the dough with slices of Bufala. Her cowl-neck
opening to her perfect bust, a nip of black lace
is dusted with flour. The light of the future
softens her skin, swirls up through her hair,

like fire, makes a double shadow on the tile,
one upright, the other bent in prayer.
Her fingertips are wet,
it isn't, but could be, blood.
Let's go there,
Sophia Loren is making a pizza,
if you dare.

Herding Rabbits

Isabel Gaddis

Waffles over the bridge,
what's done is done.

We make a side trip to the house with the rabbit hutch in the driveway.
The bunnies don't come out.

I check the web page to see
if there's a good talk at the new age bookstore
but it's some
guy.

When I drive, first I notice I've clenched my jaw, my hands, my shoulders,
and then
I realize I'm bracing
to wake up in an emergency room
with somebody in scrubs
being mean to me.

Mom has bronchitis, so we email
back and forth. They brought her dinner
on a tray,
plus a Reese's Cup,
'cause it's Halloween.
(A stroller in my Taco Bell is filled with marigolds.)

I'm ready for everyone else
to be away
for a while
so I can get
nothing
done.
Maybe sit
on the bridge
and watch the waffles
float by.

Glenn Gould

Glen Armstrong

I listen to my shoes.
And dream of a place so big.
That I am hiding wherever.
I am.
The postal carrier arrives.
I leave most of the envelopes.
Unopened.
And worry that the chicken bones.
In the roadside garbage can.
Speak of a savagery.

From which I have yet to evolve.
Some folks would rather solve.
Mysteries than eat rotisserie.
Chicken.
Some folks listen to Glenn.
Gould and only hear.
The little yelps.
And guttural yearnings.
That helped him coax big music.
From a little piano.

Fall Color Colorado
Yue Li
oil on canvas
24x18

Wedding Day
Yue Li
pastel on paper
24x18

Angels Smile
Yue Li
oil on canvas
11x14

Trees in Mongolia

James Sullivan

Irving dragged leaves into a pile in the yard, thinking he ought to start bagging soon. But then again, he had all day. Sniffing at his coat collar, he wondered why his wife couldn't smoke clove cigarettes instead. They smelled and tasted better, so why these cheap, nauseating brands? And why was she sneaking smokes—and in *his* jacket? Some Freudian self-sabotage. Another pile of leaves, raked more quickly than before, assembled on the lawn, and then he combined the two piles into one crunchy brown mass. Through the window he could see his wife, Jane, peering at something on her computer. While Irving was grateful for a mindless task, just something to do, she was more content to stay in cyberspace. But he got it.

Irving looked at that window until he saw not what was behind it but what was reflected. He saw himself standing beside a mound of what might well have seemed triceratops dung from her view, dropped dead center in a yard encircled with a white plastic fence. It couldn't even have been wood, could it. On the other side of this flimsy plastic border reflected behind him were children on their way to that school Jane and he had looked at before buying their house, the school that would have been nice. The kids chattered away, clad in wool finer than they understood. Irving felt like a break—he took a lot of breaks—so he stood watching his wife laughing at her computer as the reflected image of the world walked across her face, all of them laughing and playing.

With a sudden impulse, he jumped the neighbors' fence and started raking their leaves, frantic like a first-time thief. That house was big, and they did have one of those surveillance cameras at the front door. After the dinner party where he'd drunk a little extra, said that thing that hadn't made them laugh like he thought it would, *I mean it was a joke*, it would be awkward to explain jumping their fence. So he moved quickly. When the pile had grown, he hurled it, scattering jagged brown fragments in an arc over his fence. Several children stood at the fence watching as Irving leapt the fence again and raked the neighbors' leaves into his own pile, making the most monstrous mountain of leaves anyone present had ever seen. Irving felt pretty good just then. Work should, he thought, lead to something concrete, a growing, tangible prize. Something good to share.

"Any of you kids wanna jump in this pile?" he asked.

Two boys in blazers ran away. Those who remained, two boys and a girl, smiled and looked around for social cues.

"We have to go to school," a girl said.

"Oh, I understand. But I guess you don't want to see a Mongolian leaf worm, in that case."

"What's mom goalie and leaf worm?"

"*Mongolian* leaf worm. From Mon*golia*. They're a foot long, bright red, and as fat as a loaf of bread. And they eat ten pounds of leaves a day. That's why I'm building this pile."

"Do they even *have* trees in Mongoalie-uh?"

"Oh sure. Lots of trees but not much else. The people there are poor and hungry, but it makes some of them fight real hard. The leaf worms eat leaves all day, grow big and fat and strong, and then the Mongolian sumo wrestlers eat *them*, and they grow big and fat and strong, too."

"Yeah, *right*."

"That's why all the sumo champs in Japan are Mongolians. It's the secret source of their power. But," he said, pausing to build anticipation, "I managed to get some from my cousin."

After a moment, the girl asked, "Do you really have one?"

"I'd better have one, 'cuz my wife over there in the window, see, she's counting on having one for dinner." He pointed to Jane in the window, face embedded in leaf mountain, crunching on a piece of toast. The children watched with interest, perhaps imagining the flesh of a great worm entering her hungry mouth. "We've been on a budget these days, so we're eating them instead of steaks since summer. And I have to say, I feel strong as a silverback gorilla." He flexed under his coat and lifted the rake in the air like a dumbbell several times for effect. There was the smoke smell again. *Had* she wanted him to notice?

"You *eat* them?" the girl asked.

"Just like the sumo wrestlers. Gotta eat something."

Shaking the pile from the back side with his foot, Irving simulated movement in the leaves.

"Eat one, though, and I guarantee you'll be the strongest kids around."

"Bill Livingston's the strongest kid in my class," a boy said.

"Would you like to be stronger than him?"

The boys murmured to each other, something about dodgeball.

Irving rubbed his nose, smoky fingers.

"Some of those Mongolians, you know, they get rich and famous, but even still, it's hard to act like the Japanese. They look different, talk different, even walk a little different. Even after they work so hard for so long, crossing entire oceans to find a new home, things get hard and stressful, and sometimes they're bad, or they can't hold their rank. Why, just this year, a grand champion cracked the skull of his underling, and they gave him the boot. Have you thought hard about what to do if you get stronger? Gotta use it right. Can't go cracking skulls. Gotta stay in the game."

A breeze rustled the leaves, and the kids were quiet.

"I'll tell you what," Irving said. "I've been breeding and raising them in the garage, so I've got extras enough to share. I'm in a generous mood, so if you catch one, I'll let you keep it. They make good pets, I hear. You can even walk 'em on a leash if you're careful not to let the extra set of teeth they've got in their rear side nibble your toes."

"They bite!?"

"Only little nips here and there. The teeth are only sharp enough to chomp leaves, so it doesn't hurt much. But see, the thing is, if you wanna get them to come out, you've gotta come up running and shouting and jump right in the pile."

"Are you for real?" a boy said.

"Are you chicken?" Irving replied.

"I dunno."

"Buckaw!"

Two boys and a girl burst into the yard, pushing and laughing, then shouting and jumping into the mountain of leaves and Mongolian leaf worms. Irving grabbed two armfuls of leaves and tossed them into the air above the laughing kids. The kids followed suit, diving in and out of leaves and casting leaves all across the yard.

"There aren't any worms in here!" a boy said.

"Yeah, you got me."

"Grown-ups aren't supposed to lie!"

"Oh, really? I learn new things every day!" Irving dumped an armful of leaves over the boy's head, and the boy fired back with two little handfuls of his own.

Jane watched from the window. Irving smiled at her, but she returned only a tired expression. She soon appeared at the front door in a robe, cigarette in hand. She lit up as Irving came up to meet her, kids still playing in the yard, blue blazers a backdrop for orange and brown. She blew a sibilant stream toward the Mongolian leaf worms, and for a long time, neither of them said anything. They watched as the children played within their plastic fence, their world of fictions and leaves.

Beethoven's Piano

AKaiser-Veyrat

for EKV

We were frequent company you and me,
your resonant friend, when so many others had grown
tired of your deaf ringing stare, notebooks to fill.
You, tired of their emptying moving mouths. That shock
of hair was a nice touch, of course, and it fell
on your dampened forehead as you moved for Elise,
the key to your patience. Over and over again
those same sounds. I did my best. I know about love,
too, you know. I also know about dead air.
When you are gone, it seeps into my hollowed space
like lesions on an eardrum. When you are out,
the star at a public airing, and have to be turned around
to see fevered hands, clapping. All in all, I'd say
we've done pretty well. Counterpoint obsessions our
own panacea. I've learned to live your moods,
my weeping thunder. You've played me like no other.

Opals

Carrie Greenlaw

Opals are beautiful and unlucky—
so which is it?

Gleaming bones inlaid with chipped rainbow:
ocher, aquamarine, and a faint pink
casting light under my knuckle.

He once broke his hand punching
a theater seat—she stopped loving him
but kept loving other people.
Now his finger tilts drunkenly askew,
like a glissando.

Sometimes we fuck like strangers;
after sex he says it won't always be this good
but I couldn't care less.
We won't always pass for young.
This house won't always smell like us.
Someday it will be my ashes and his corpse
or his ashes and my corpse.

Life is beautiful and temporary—
so which is it?

I wear my opals to the symphony.
Friday the 13th. I stack bad luck
on bad luck.

Dimitri is weeping in the basement.
The Soviet composers are still fleeing in their graves,
suitcases packed and rotting under the mattress,
but the black horseshoe onstage slings hope after fevered hope,
turns us all into ghosts tonight.

Blue Note: A Road Trip Sestina

Marc Meierkort

Car radio serves morning gospels
as if church were a way to escape the lure of the dial,
its tendency to throw off suffering like the blues.
Music holds these human remains out of tune,
muffled in a dying breath, deaf & blind,
left dangling off the pin-drop of return.

He swims through stars, offers to return
his penance of policy & philosophy on the gospels,
pitches a theory of temptation's blind
spot knowledge behind the static dial.
Bottleneck voices fade out of tune.
He submits to color, something about blue

egos & failed music. He sleeps inside the blue
facade pulled over slight indecision. The return
reaction of light, like stars, searches for a tune
not far removed from time's insistence on the gospel.
Slow-motion hands finger the fragile dial.
He catches the yellow-line stare, falls blind.

Falling behind he leaves his eyes to the blind
slow notes of jazz, slow boat of the blues.
Designed to travel empty distances, he dials
up a site where silence need not be returned.
His nest of doubting faith cringes into gospel.
His car rocks against the shoulder, falls into tune.

He steps over bright water to reel in the tune
transmitted across light's way of looking, the blind
dalliance (damnation ranted at members of a gospel)
forever entombed beside the belief of blue
memory, blue notes ascribed as blasphemy returned.
No right. No wrong. Just something left of the dial.

He cannot recall any name without a spinning dial.
He never submits a frequency better set in tune.
Nothing harbors light quite like salt-return.
No one shelters blood. No one sings the blues.
He cannot preserve flesh for the feast of the gospel.
He cannot hide behind that which was never blind.

Car radio dials up stations of the cross. The blind
stop on a tune, feel their flesh melt into blue.
He promises to return. New blood. A new gospel.

Side B: Album Cut

Marc Meierkort

I

Rhyme begins with the sword & the pen,
arcane structures kneading Now to Then.

Pop culture lionizes names, cubic refrains,
church hymns margined with passive ink stains.

We hold onto Lowell & Whitman's *Leaves of Grass*
for door prizes & Herb Alpert's Tijuana Brass

gone bathing in pools of indulgence & sin
drowned in a backwash of bathtub gin.

II

Rhyme put down the pen
if only between then
& the foreshadowing of never again.

Glass shards hurled
into the air
& called the moon

freeze inside stone chipped

& marked bone where marrow
turns to subtle erasures of record.

Angel-driven & calling for love,
shattering stars fired God's determination,
proof in death that mind maneuvers body.

III

Rhyme put down the sword
between the ladies & lords,
held back the barbarians. Bored

elements of reminiscence
engulf the agency toward ritual dance,
insinuations in cartilage

that chivalry affords shelter
from the swelter of giving one's blood
to the cause of religious floodwaters.

Blind imitation surrounds & bottles
& drains Andy Warhol down the sewer
where human waste resembles faith.

The Round House of Love, and Not

Kelly R. Samuels

Bini's La Cupola and Gordon's Xanadu

Begin with the shape. It will give you access: this. This dome the color of dry sand with its sea view. This mound reminiscent of the cave, from late Latin, meaning small cask or vault, diminutive of cupa. How no corners? This always threw me. From far back—that time in her round house in northern Minnesota, all the tongue and groove and rooms like slices of pie. I wanted the perpendicular, the sharp edge, even then. In the picture of the stairs, those granite slabs, there is an edge. I imagine descending, minding my tread. Me, having caught myself just in time that time on Hunter's Point. Lovers and their houses, their love nests. This one for three years when I was learning to walk and ask for an apple.

Later, I was taken to that one of the future, bright white
and less solid. Its great room bloomed into another and another,
windows like windshields. It felt like a roadside attraction, was
a roadside attraction that lasted as long as it takes for cells to
renew. Too, that benchmark of marriage. The guide shared it was
begun in that cruelest of months, the one I was born in, and my friend
with her crocheted poncho nudged me and snickered.
There's a picture of me standing by the polyurethane tree looking
as if I thought there was no future. Or: this was all it would look
like. Maybe I had an inkling of that winter later still, when I passed
through. The roller coasters, their rails bent reeds of unfinished
baskets edged in snow. Their precariousness startled. I recalled my
mother's story of the girl at the fair, the unlatched door, plummet.
Another kind of fall, no slippery stone, but rather grasp.

This house. That house. One in disrepair. One no longer.
Both were made with balloons, plastic or of the sky.

The Unpublished Poems of Marilyn Monroe

Susana H. Case

She thought it important to be photographed
book in hand. Marilyn
in a striped swimsuit reading *Ulysses*
(shot by Eve Arnold, 1955).
Blondes can be sexy *and* astute.

Blonde, pejorative: nineteenth century,
as in *dizzy blonde*; as in
risqué British burlesque
performer; as in French courtesan
Rosalie Duthé; as in *a blonde moment*.

Marilyn left fragments of handwritten texts,
sincerity in her crossed-out words,
inserted phrases. Memories,
dreams, fears—enjambed.
The public knew the lines of her cupid's bow,
the emotional sway of her upper lip.
Would a silly woman stand by Arthur Miller
as he refused to name Communists?

Marilyn, surrounded by 430 books
with penciled notes, writes to herself:
ah life they / have cheated you

The Clouds Were the Reason

Sarah Brown Weitzman

I moved to Florida
white jagged Alps
on the western horizon

I am driving toward
but can never reach
later dropping rain so dense
the world blurs.

Or discrete morning clouds
suggestive shapes leaving gaps
of blue
like cut outs
in a censored letter.

Just before dusk back-lit wisps
reflect the lowering sun

as exhausted day drags itself
over the twelve mountains
of hours.

Later lightning zigzags
across the sky like a crack
in a boiled egg
chased by thunder.

Take cover.

Volcano
Sandy Coomer
acrylic pour painting on gessobord
8x16

The Flowers

Kody Stadler

"The bell on the weather teleprinter rang 12 times, and police dispatcher Marc Hood spun around from the radio console to see what was so important. Topeka had been under a tornado watch since before noon and it was now near 7, but Officer Hood wasn't concerned.

"He had sat out many watches since joining the Topeka Police Department in 1959. On tornado days the weather is hot and sultry, and black clouds boil and hang low above the ground. Today had dawned with a damp coolness that had reminded the dispatcher of September. But he didn't believe in taking chances.

"He tore off the message, a warning of the approach of a thunderstorm. It must be looking a little rough outside, he thought, because cars were asking permission to go up on TV Hill at the western edge of the city to watch for funnels from the west.

"Lieut. Robert Martin, senior patrol officer on duty, came in to ask about the weather and the two of them then studied the bureau's message. It was time, they decided, to put out what Topeka police call 'the weather watch.'"

—*The National Observer*, 1967

***

She smelled like flowers in the morning, before the bloom. Sometimes I spent entire days trying to figure out which flowers made me think of her. At first, they were roses; later, daisies. Today, I thought of stargazer lilies—pink and white, just like her blouse, while the petals of her hair curled gently towards her body. Her name is Maddie Fitzpatrick, and when she laughs, I am the bee that follows her call, careful not to ruin her fragile beauty with all of my poison. I've had a crush on her since the first time I saw her in my freshman year of high school. Four years later, I've now graduated with a degree and missed opportunities.

Normally, I already would have seen her this morning, but summer has arrived, so there is only work and heat. Today is cooler than most, however, and I head to the Westboro Cleaners accompanied by a sly cloudy sky. I pray for storms on my way to work, so that I may see her in the rain later. She has always loved the rain, and it makes her smile more than anything else I've ever seen—except for when her art professor had said her painting was admitted into a small museum on our college campus in the city. It was of a bird, nestling itself into the warmth of an oak tree she had seen in my front yard.

***

"On June 8, 1966, [...] Marc Hood was going through all the proper motions, but he was sure nothing would happen. Nevertheless, at 6:55 p.m., he began transmitting to the police cars, dispatching them to five vantage points around the city. He ticked them off from memory:

"'Car 43, at the municipal golf course, 21st west, would you take up the weather watch?'

"Car 43: 'Okay. We've been going up on WIBW [TV] Hill.'

"Hood: '109 is on top of the hill. It is 6:56.'

"Hood: 'Car 108. Would you take up a position somewhere near Goodyear where you can see out north? It is 6:57.'

"Hood: 'Car 107, go over by the turnpike entrance on Highway 75 for weather.'

"That took care of the west, northwest, north, and south. All that remained was Burnett's Mound on the southwest corner of town. It was the best, if riskiest, viewpoint for tornados.

"Hood: 'Car 45?'

"Car 45: 'I'm on the mound.'"

—*The National Observer*, 1967

***

"Hello? Hello? Hey! Johnny! Quit your daydreaming, goddammit, we got a job to do! Now, come on, this is a good client, we gotta go to the west side of town."

Jack McAllister, my boss, is a 50-year-old man with 70 years' worth of grudges. He once told me that if he had a nickel for everyone he had ever wanted to fight, he would have burned Westboro Cleaners to the ground years ago, and I would be just another unemployed high school graduate while he lived in luxury out by the West Coast. He later told me that if he had a quarter for everyone he had actually fought, however, he would have enough to pay for a dollar of his medical bills. When I asked him why he had changed the amount of money he got for each person, he told me to get back to work and stop asking questions.

"Aw hell," he said, glancing over to his left side as we drove down 21st Street to our client's house. "They're just tearing that goddamned thing apart."

The "thing" that he was referring to was Burnett's Mound, one of the highest points of land in our city. Five years before, the city had decided to start construction for an interstate bypass, starting with a water tank that now bulged its way outward on the north side of the mound for all of us to see—a testament to our war with nature. According to some of the locals, it was considered a sacred ground by the Chief Abram B. Burnett and his tribe of Potawatomie natives, protected by wind spirits that continued to save us from evil.

"That's the thing about some of these city folk that I'll never understand. They just take something beautiful and piss on it, all for the sake of convenience. Then, when it bites them in the ass, they turn around and sue everyone they can to get out of it. Why can't we just leave well enough alone?"

"Didn't you say you would move to the West Coast if you ever got rich? There ain't nothing but city people out there."

"Oh, please," Jack scoffs. "Like where?"

"California, for starters."

"Ha ha! See, that's the difference!"

"What?"

"California's already a hellhole. All's we gotta do is soak up the rays."

***

"Some Topekans recount a legend that Burnett's Mound would keep tornadoes from striking. The Weather Bureau said this had been disproved many times, but still the storms that had hit Topeka had never caused great damage.

"On Burnett's Mound, Hathaway saw something like a black finger dip down from the cloud. It pulled back up. A second time the finger dipped and pulled back. Then a third time.

"'It was just like you dropped your little finger, then pulled it back up,' Hathaway said."

—Elon Torrence, 1966

***

We worked until our bodies began to open and surrender themselves to the ground. Although the sky was cool in the morning, the heat soon came and pushed its way into our souls until we could take the strain no longer. I left my body and daydreamt of flowers blooming, while she and I collapsed in the field together, far away from summer and our tumorous futures. I often fear what's next to come in our lives; I don't know where to go, or what to do. The only thing I'm sure of is her, but what if she leaves?

In my daydream, she tells me to come with her to New Mexico, where she recently got accepted to the Santa Fe University of Art and Design, one of the most prestigious art schools in the region.

"But what'll I do?" I ask her.

"I don't know," she replies. "But we'll figure it out—together."

"Goddammit, boy, what did I tell you?" Jack wheezes, as the fields around me suddenly vanish. "Come on; get your head out of the clouds."

Jack leans over and coughs violently into a piece of cloth as we pack up to leave. He would never admit it to anyone, but his time is almost over. He, too, dreams of fields and flowers, and pretty girls to lie next to within them, but is instead met with dust, dirt, and chemicals. Maybe that's why he's so sensitive to the desecration of Burnett's Mound, I often wonder—because they both have been ruined by the demands of those around them.

***

"The tornado hit with full force at 25th & Randolph missing the KNI complex but leveling homes and smashing apartment building[s] in a three block wide area bounded by Randolph, 21st Street, College, and Shunga Drive.

"Odor of gas permeated the area; wires were down; trees, cars, household goods, walls and roofs were mashed together in a hopeless goulash of destruction.

"A woman was pinned beneath a chimney in a house in the 2300 block of High but walked to safety when freed by civilians. Four elderly people were taken from houses in the 2200 block of High, their faces caked with a compound of mud and blood.

"Another elderly woman lay moaning in intense pain on a mattress in her living room in the 2200 block [of] High, the roof over her head vanished, the four walls sagging about her. She was removed with about six other injured and taken to city hospitals in a camper truck manned by civilians.

"Teenagers from south of the Shunga Creek came across to aid in evacuation. None of the houses in this area were habitable. About half were leveled and the other half showing only bare walls standing against the angry sky.

"[The] homes with storm shelters were clogged full of neighbors, many with small children, who could be heard screaming above the thunder of the twister."

—Jack Kenward, 1966

***

I finally make it home and call out for my parents, but am only greeted with the creaks of an empty house and the distant lullaby of a thunderstorm. I wonder what Maddie is thinking and if she is also listening to the thunderstorm with me, though in another place—two lovers staring at the same moon with gushing eyes. Once in my room, I close my eyes and dream of being back with her and the flowers, now safe in the comfort of solitude, and with the roar of the thunderstorm growing louder; I am in another place with another me.

In this world, I am strong and brave, and I walk right up to Maddie Fitzpatrick and ask her to be mine. She blushes shades of pink—just like a stargazer lily—and softly replies, yes, and, in this world, I now lift her face to mine with fingers underneath her chin, and lean in for a kiss. I am no longer afraid, no longer lost, and Santa Fe and New Mexico and the world are ours to explore together.

***

"A beautiful lady was attacked, beaten, battered and scarred last Wednesday night. Her name was Topeka. But she will recover—to new and more magnificent beauty. Meantime, she will suffer in her recuperation.

"Old timers will remember the legend of Indian Chief Burnett, and the remarkable 'Burnett's Mound,' which was supposed to provide 'trade winds' to fight off the tornadoes trying to attack the queen city of Kansas. Something happened last Wednesday night. The legend didn't work.

"Educated and rational people pooh-poohed the idea a tornado would ever strike the Capital City. In over 100 years of history, no damaging tornado ever had. Before Wednesday night.

"And then out of the blackness of a howling banshee of a cloud, destruction bore down upon the city with a speed which recalled the lines of the old hymn, 'His Terrible Swift Sword,' a devastation to try the very sanity of those caught in the path."

—Bert Carlyle, 1966

***

In the middle of the dream, I notice a shift and I am suddenly in another. This dream does not take place in flowers, however; it takes place in the night. I am floating in the sky, wading through the stars like they're all a part of one big lake—the biggest lake I've ever seen in my life. Far away, I see my grandparents; a boy that jumped off the Kansas Avenue bridge; childhood pets. I wave to them and ask how they are, but get no response back. They are all staring at me with a solemnness that I cannot describe.

Then, even farther, I see her. But she is not looking at me. She is looking towards the bottom, and crying. I want to reach over and comfort her, to wipe away her tears and tell her everything will be okay. But this is another world now, and I am not brave. I am not strong. I am not another me anymore. I'm just me.

***

“The sky that evening was unforgettable. I’ve never seen weather like it before or since. The sky churned green and yellow, and then the air was deathly still. There was no doubt in anyone’s mind that a serious storm was developing. The adults were listening to a portable radio. When they heard that a tornado had touched down near Burnett’s Mound and was headed our way, they herded us into the temple’s basement.

“The next day’s newspaper carried photos of the carnage. A neighbor, John Scheibe, was dead. He had just graduated from high school a day or two before the storm. We later heard from his family that he’d been asleep alone at home. Apparently the storm did not waken him. He was found ‘wrapped around a tree’ in his front yard. He had a severe head injury. He was taken to the hospital, but never regained consciousness and died within a few hours. His mother’s hair literally turned white overnight.”

—Carol Yoho, 2006

REFERENCES

"Burnett's Mound: Story and Legend." *Chief Abram B. Burnett Family.* N.p., n.d. Web. 4 Nov. 2016.

Carlyle, Bert. "The Queen Now Carries Ugly Scars." *The Topeka Capital-Journal.* N.p., June 1966. Web. 4 Nov. 2016.

Kenward, Jack. "Storm Hits in Randolph." *The Topeka Capital-Journal.* N.p., June 1966. Web. 4 Nov. 2016.

M, Ralph. "'The Clouds Were Doing Strange Things in the Sky Above the Valley'" *The National Observer.* N.p., 12 June 1967. Web. 4 Nov. 2016.

Yoho, Carol. "Personal Topeka Tornado Stories." *Stories of the '66 Topeka Tornado*. KTWU, n.d. Web. 4 Nov. 2016.

American Family

Carrie La Seur

My nieces' eyes are brown and sweet as dates,
their arms warm cords around my neck,
black curls soft as brushing olive branches
in Amman.

We wait for sunset

to eat lamb together, with mint
and Sam Salad, named
for their daddy who makes it.

His names have become new.
They bend to an American shape,
foreign to the sounds he whispers
to his daughters. Inshallah.

We sit at a table of four languages.
Tortillas, sourdough, pita, baguette.
We mumble prayers, hold tight:

Protect this family.

God of my Puritan ancestors:
God of adobe churches in Zacapa:
God of Mecca, God most high:
Protect this my American family.

Thoughts on Staircases

Kelly R. Samuels

There are three in this house even if one is never or rarely used. The dank narrow well that once must have been the coal chute. The second with its wonky third-to-last step you have said you would fix for seven years now, that I always claim I'll meet my death on or: at the bottom of. And the third we carpeted leading to the second floor, to the rooms with the views of the tops of trees and their shadows being cast early morning and late in the day. Three that some say are home to spirits, those smudgy apparitions that do not, cannot go the way of, but rather stay. Waiting or wakened to greet us with a chill or sudden foreboding or sadness or anger—whichever the person felt in their last minutes. For: not happiness. Nor contentment. Maybe peace, though it never feels like that here. The one man we know died in this house did not go gently and certainly is found in the first. I cannot seem to ascend or descend fast enough on those six steps with both doors swinging shut, thrusting me into darkness. And though I must take my time on the second set, something/someone is there, too. Or perhaps: my own glimpse of—the jokes about Millay really not all that funny. Only the third so steep and yet leading to light calms me, and more often than not, I am found sitting on the top step, or right in the middle reading or thinking or considering options—where to finally go and when.

After the Bingo Game

Louisa Howerow

Pioneer Home, February

I walk my mother into the night, the falling snow,
leave behind the rec room, the door we tap-code
to exit-enter. Cold narrows her breath. Little wonder.

Mucus-filled lungs push at her chest, barely. I hear
again about the indoor smell, the dullness. I'm waiting
for my ping of guilt. What if I came more often?

The downside: we'd end up hating each other. A cage
takes on so many shapes, often doesn't open—rib cage,
bird cage, fight cage. Balls roll out from a bingo cage,

at random, but she believes in auspicious numbers.
Lucky six, she kept chanting. Her last card, one number
for a blackout, a chance to call out BINGO!

An ambulance wails. "I'm still here," she says,
and we know this time *here* means alive. We laugh,
hers more of a wheeze. Intermittent gusts of wind

swirl the top of piled snow. She reaches for her hat,
then mine, makes sure they're still both on. "Crystal headdress.
Snegurochka," she uses the diminutive for Snow Maiden.

Her arm in mine, our steps shuffling in rhythm, we round
the Home's gazebo, back to the door. I start to brush her coat,
and she stops me. "Feathers, better still. We're snow geese."

How a Poem Is Like a Rube Goldberg

Sarah Brown Weitzman

It begins with an idea attached to a phrase
that nudges an image
that falls on a line of memories
like dominoes tripping a series of images
that strike another string of images
which upsets the balance of a ball
of meanings sending them down
the funnel of experience
picking up a universal thereby
tilting the cage of language
thus igniting a rocket of understanding
setting off an avalanche
of words spooling out
and unwinding even more words
that start feelings that open
a gate which releases something
entirely new that strikes
a bell that rings and rings
until the poem is summoned

THE LANDSCAPE A 2572018
Andrew Foster
spray paint on poster board
28x22

The One With The Faces A 1972018
Andrew Foster
spray paint on pizza box lid
16x16

The Girl A 482018
Andrew Foster
spray paint on poster board
14x22

Sisterhood

Katy Mullins

My sister Holly had a box underneath her bed that held all of the different things she'd stolen. Some nights, Holly would pull the box out from under our bunk bed to show me the latest treasures she'd acquired—a ring she'd stolen from a friend, a piece of candy she'd lifted from the drugstore. The box was only about a foot long, two inches deep at most. In my mind it's always larger: the size of our bed, the size of our dresser, the size of the entire room. Holly's secrets took up more space than she did. They became my secrets too, filling the corners and drifting around the ceiling so that even when she was elsewhere, echoes of her remained, whispering from the little box under our bed.

Holly was most proud of the necklace she'd stolen right after her sixteenth birthday, a necklace she'd given as a gift to herself. I was fourteen and had grown two inches over the previous year. Neither of my parents had been able to afford a new coat for me, let alone a gift for her.

At the time, my mother and father were both still adjusting to the new life they had created for themselves. Or rather, the life my father had created for them. He had just lost his job working in a lumber yard, and in a moment of mania, he took our savings and made an offer to the owner of the bakery down the street, a tiny frail woman after whom Betsy's Bakery was named. And that was that, the bakery was theirs—ours. My mother was very quiet when he told us. He was talking fast, too fast, excitement jumbling his words against his teeth. Bits of chicken flinging from his mouth. Landing in glistening tan flecks on the table cloth. The tines of my mother's fork scraped vegetables around her plate in the pause that followed. Those small squeaks were the most she ever said about it. She quit her teaching position the next day, and the day after that, she and my father were standing side by side behind the counter, selling bread and smiling.

That night—the night of Holly's sixteenth birthday—my mother woke me up around one in the morning. Her thin hands reached up to my bunk and shook my shoulders.

"Wake up. Get dressed."

She kept shaking me, the bony tips of her fingers burying into my shoulder blade. I blinked. My room was very dark, the hint of morning still far away. I could see my mother's eyes reflecting in the darkness, the square light from the window curving around the upper part of her irises. She pressed some clothes into my lap and stepped back so I could climb down.

"What's happening?" I asked, pressing my knuckles to my eyes, but her footsteps were already on the stairs.

I swung my feet out of bed, reaching with my toes to feel down to the next rung of the bunk ladder. It was a chilly summer night. My palms were on my mattress and I could still feel where my body had been, a warm silhouette pressed into the sheets. Holly's bed was cold as I sat down to pull on socks and shoes. Outside, a car engine started, growling to life among the gentle waves of cricket chirps. I stepped out into the cool night air and hurried toward the car, which was idling next to the basketball hoop that sat at the end of our cul-de-sac. Holly was already in the passenger seat so I swung myself into the back. My mother hit the gas, and we sped around the loop and up Magnolia Lane.

Holly had fallen out of a tree. She'd broken her arm in three places, according to the ER doctor who had gauges in his ears and walked on the balls of his feet. It took only a few hours to set her arm, and we drove back home under the stars. Her arm was in a fresh blue cast that stretched from elbow to wrist and captured her two smallest fingers as well. She had it crossed over her body, folded her right arm across the plaster. She'd had to take off the bracelets she usually wore, the peace signs and jelly bands and leather braids. She'd doubled them up on her other wrist instead, so that they stretched clear down her forearm, nearly to her elbow, looking almost like a second cast. She stretched out in her bed when we got home, lying on her back with her arms folded over her chest.

"Why were you in a tree?" I asked. I was leaning over the edge of the railing, my feet hooked into the opposite side of the top bunk so I wouldn't topple off. Holly wasn't looking at me but rather directly above her, into the underside of my bunk. She reached up with the hand that was not broken and pushed her hair out of her face.

"I was visiting Adam," she said. He was her latest boyfriend. They'd been together a month. Holly had told me the day before that she was going to marry him when she was old enough. She'd also said the same about the last three boys she dated. "I just fell on my way down."

"Like climbing out his window?"

She smiled. I could see her white teeth in the darkness. "I got something though." She rolled and reached underneath her bunk, extracting the box from under the frame. She sat up, fumbling with the lid, trying to hold the box between her cast and her body as she lifted an edge of the top. She slid her fingers into the opening. Bead by bead, the lid of the box bumping over every individual sphere, she pulled out a long, glowing pearl necklace.

"It was in his mother's jewelry box," she said. "I swiped it right out of their room." She had been speaking softly, but her voice got swept slightly higher on a current of excitement.

I was still hanging over the edge of my bed, the frame cold on my palms. I reached down, holding my breath. Holly held the necklace up to me. My heart thudded between my mattress and my spine, beating beneath my ribs and in my ears. I rolled the pearls through my fingers, feeling how they grew in size as they got closer to the center of the necklace. I'd seen Holly's stash before, but she rarely let me hold one of the things she kept inside. "Does Mom know?"

"No," she said. "I didn't tell her where I was." She looked up at me. "Don't you dare snitch."

I rolled my eyes and pulled myself back into my bed. I had just started to drift off to sleep when I heard our door open and our father's heavy footsteps. He'd spent the past three days—and nights—in the bakery, nonstop. When I'd seen him earlier that day, he'd had flour in his hair, streaked through his brown waves. He hadn't slept, only eaten what my mother had told him to eat, and wouldn't talk about anything except the new recipe he was inventing for cookies.

He dragged Holly out of bed, holding the arm in the cast, swearing at her. My mother stood pressed on the side of the door, her shadow framed by the rectangle of light on the floor from the illuminated hallway. It stretched her, made her look thinner, narrower, the body in the shadow much smaller than her own. Her head was bowed. She stepped back as my father pulled Holly from the room, shutting the door until the light was nothing more than a thin line on the floor, glowing orange. I laid on my back, arms at my sides, listening to my father's distant yelling.

I don't remember falling asleep. When I woke up, Holly was already out for the day, my mother at the bakery, my father asleep in his room, his snores filling the house for the first time in days.

***

An older couple moved into the house across the street about a year later. My mother brought them a pie that they set atop a moving box in their entry way. I shook both of their hands and looked into their eyes. They were holding hands as they talked to my mother, asking about the neighborhood, about our family's bakery. Holly flashed her teeth at them when my mother introduced her, but I saw her brown eyes darting around from below her bangs, taking in the labels on the boxes: shoes, toiletries, books, decorations. She was taking inventory, looking at what they had. Meanwhile, her box continued to fill, the objects piling up like our father's cookies in the bakery. A guitar pick from the music shop next to Betsy's. A flag from a potted plant on a porch further down Magnolia Lane. A button, a thimble, a large Canadian coin.

My fifteenth birthday came on a warm day in June. My father was in the bakery all day making cookies, filling the display case, occupying both shelves in the oven. There were more cookies than we ever could have sold. I was kneading bread dough, watching him silently, flour packing under my nails and along my cuticles. Sweat tickled my back as it rolled under my shirt, condensing in the punishing heat of the ovens in the back of the bakery. I didn't want to leave but didn't want to stay either, wary of the mood my father was in. My mother came by, her quick eyes darting around as she took in the scene at hand, the multitude of cookies. She untied my apron and ushered me out the back door without a word, right past my father, who didn't look up.

I walked home, two left hand turns to get to our street, staying in the cool shade that had started to stretch over the left side of Magnolia Lane. I stopped in front of the house across the street. The front door was open and people were meandering around the side yard. A sign was tacked on the telephone pole nearby: Housewarming Party, 2-4pm.

I walked to the front porch and stepped across the threshold. My eyes took a moment to adjust to the lighting in the hallway, which was paneled with dark wood. It divided the house and led directly to the back, where I could see a few of my neighbors sitting on the porch. I stood for a moment, looking at the boxes still piled to the left of the entry way, at the couch in the living room off to my right. Voices came from the kitchen, a crisp pop as somebody opened a can of soda.

I wondered if we had gotten an invitation. I could picture my father looking at it and ripping it up in one smooth motion. I turned and started up the stairs, which were bordered by a heavy wooden banister. The upstairs hallway was dark, all the doors closed except the one that led to the master bedroom. I walked through.

The carpet of their room felt soft beneath my shoes, dappled with the late afternoon sunlight poking through the leaves of an oak tree. Boxes sat piled at the foot of the bed, which was covered by an enormous red quilt. Voices were coming through the glass doors that led to a balcony overlooking the backyard. I turned around, facing the dresser, which had a variety of objects scattered at random across the surface. A golden watch. A picture of the couple, many years younger, sitting on the back of a boat and squinting into the sun. A keychain from the Grand Canyon. My fingers grazed over a large hairbrush with a silver handle. My heartbeat was pulsing in my fingertips as I touched it, electricity sparking against the metal surface. This was the kind of possession both of them would assume the other had misplaced, a casual *hey, have you seen* that hairbrush? I slipped it into my pocket.

***

I had no idea what to do with the hairbrush. I kept moving it, putting it in the bathroom closet, then in my dresser, eventually balled into a pair of socks which I shoved below the rest. Even when I wasn't thinking about it, it still tugged at the edge of my consciousness, the guilt nipping on my heels as I walked to the bakery, swimming through my dreams on the current of Holly's gentle snores below me.

When I finally told her, Holly sat on her bed without moving. She was seventeen at the time, wore fewer bracelets and more makeup, her cheeks always an unnatural rosy pink. She crossed her legs, uncrossed them, walked to my dresser and pulled it out as though she knew right where to find it. She turned the hairbrush over in her fingers, the silver handle clinking against her rings. Her pinky had never healed properly from the break. It sat at an angle slightly crooked from her others. She wasn't smiling, but the dimple on her left cheek was showing. She pushed her hair out of her face with her palm, looking up at me from underneath her curls. Without a word, she sat back on her bed, reached under the frame, and slipped the hairbrush into the box.

***

And then it became our collection, a personal chronicle of our lives as remembered by things that did not belong to us. The fake fruit we stole from the hotel lobby during our Las Vegas vacation. The only vacation our family took in my teenage years, in fact, and only because our father booked it in the middle of the night and presented us with the plane tickets scheduled to leave the following morning. A golden cufflink from that vacation too, found on the seat of a bus that had just been vacated by a man in a suit, concealed in Holly's back pocket until we could slide it into our luggage. We delighted in how easy it was. We knew how little certain things would be missed. We took a dog collar from a friend at a fourth of July barbeque, lifted silver earrings from our aunt's jewelry box at Christmas. We drove our father's old and battered Toyota to the mall, drifted in and out of stores, slipping bracelets into our pockets and tucking trinkets under our clothes. We never took a lot, never talked about it before or afterward. It was a museum of moments collected entirely in silence. As though the thrill, the spell that stealing cast over us, would be shattered the instant either of us spoke of it.

Holly added things faster than I could: a shoelace, a whistle, a single knitting needle. The box became full enough that the lid no longer stayed on properly. It demanded more space in my mind as well, always in the shadows behind my thoughts. My eyes never rested in one location for long, always looking for the next thing I could take, the next thing that might become ours.

My mother lost some weight. Her head stayed bowed so often that it looked like she was retreating into her hair, which was going gray and became limp around her high cheekbones. My father installed a double oven in the bakery and spent hours, days, baking and baking.

One night, the summer before Holly was going to leave for college, she said, "We should stop."

I had been drifting to sleep, listening to the drops of rain pricking the window, but I was abruptly alert, focused. For a moment, neither of us inhaled. I felt that deflating sensation in my shoulders, in my chest, coupled with a nervous jumping of my heart.

"Why?"

The rain became louder, like pebbles on the glass. My ears were straining against the clatter of the droplets, against the rushing blood in my ears, to hear her answer. My breathing even felt too loud.

"I almost got caught when I took that deck of cards. You should stop too." Her sentences were chopped, a finality in the last one. I could almost hear her place the period at the end of her warning, a final puff of air.

A few days later I came down the stairs, wandering into the kitchen for a snack, when the scene in front of me caused me to pull up short, stopping in the shadow of the doorframe. The rest of my family was seated around the table in our kitchen, an oddly displaced piece of furniture that would have been better suited for a patio. The wooden slats that formed the table top sitting a quarter inch apart so that the floor was visible between the gaps. Dad sat in the middle, Holly and my mother on either side. On the table directly in front of him was the box.

I didn't recognize it at first. I'd only ever seen it in our room. As if it could only exist there. As if the box, by definition, had to remain under Holly's bed, as if moving it would transform it into something else. To see it in another space was wrong, impossible.

Holly was running her fingers over the pinky on her other hand, the one she'd broken, the one that was still crooked. My mother's face was concealed by her hair. My father had his hands on either side of the box, holding it like a plate of food he was preparing to consume. I couldn't discern his expression; it was filled with conflicting features. His brows were heavy over his eyes, anger in the creases. But his lips were parted slightly. I could just see the bottoms of his front teeth, almost in smile. As if he was amused. Or, for some reason, feeling just the hint of delight.

"Where," he said, and then paused, his mouth working silently as he searched for the words. "Where on Earth did you learn it's okay to steal?" His voice was exaggerated, his tongue rolling around each syllable, shaping the words so deliberately that Holly could not miss a single moment. He dumped the box on the table, running his fingers through the glinting objects. My mother sat farther back in her chair, arms across her chest, pressed into the hollow of her stomach so that her elbows were in line with her rib cage, as if she could sink backward further and become the chair itself. I watched from the doorframe, not moving. He picked up a book, one that we'd taken from our cousin's baby shower. I could hear his heavy breathing as he let it fall open in his hand, holding it away from his body as though repulsed by it. In one fluid motion, he snapped it shut, pulled his arm back, and hurled it at Holly. It spun through the air and she ducked, throwing her arms over her face. The corner clipped her arm, drawing blood.

Holly said, when we were back in our room later, that she thought he enjoyed those moments where he was allowed to unleash his temper. He'd yelled so that spittle gathered at the corners of his mouth, which he would lick away with his tongue. She was holding a paper towel over her arm.

"You didn't say anything," she said. "I saw you in the doorway." One of her bracelets slid lower down her arm, past the cut, dragging a small streak of blood with it.

"What was I supposed to do?" I said. My face was flushing, the heat crawling up my neck.

Holly stared at me and I stared at her. Then she stood and walked out of our room, leaving me lying in her bed.

***

There was no box under our bed anymore, no single storage space for the objects, but they accumulated on her side of the room anyway. Earrings that had gone out of style a decade ago, the posts rusted, sitting on top of her jewelry box. A pair of jeans several sizes too big for her draped across the bottom of the bed frame. A flannel shirt with the anti-theft tags still in place.

Holly was leaving for college soon. The things continued to clutter her side, piling up on her dresser and at the foot of our bunk. I told myself I'd say something, played out in my head a scene in which we sat side by side on her bed, where I told her it was too much and she agreed, found a new hobby, started baking cookies with my father or maybe tried something new, like running. I spent hours walking circles around our room, scripting my dialogue, telling myself I'd confront her tomorrow, and tomorrow, and tomorrow. But soon Holly packed for college and I still hadn't said anything.

And then the day came when we were moving Holly out, all of her belongings shoved into the trunk of our car. It was a hot August day. It was humid as well, all of us sweating through our shirts, my father's balding scalp shining in the sun. Holly's belongings filled the trunk, then the entire back seat as well. We worked for quite a while, moving the boxes in a silent parade, looping in and out of the house.

Holly and I said a clumsy goodbye, a hug where my chin bumped her shoulder and she knocked into my ear. The pearl necklace she'd stolen years before was looped around her neck, white spheres shining in the sunlight. My mother was behind the wheel as she took her spot in the passenger seat. She waved as they circled around the end of our street. I waved back, opening and closing my fingers until the car turned off Magnolia Lane.

My father had gone back inside already, the smell of cookies lingering in the air behind him. I heard the door of the house close, thought about following him inside, but decided to wait, standing in the hot sun a little longer. A breeze swept through the oak tree in our neighbor's backyard, the leaves scratching against one another. I bent to pick up something that had fallen out of Holly's pocket, clattered to the sidewalk near our feet as we'd embraced. My hair swung forward, picked up by the breeze. I stood up, shaking it out of my face to examine the object in my hands.

It was a pair of sunglasses. Sunglasses I'd recognized, black with little blue flowers along the sides. Sunglasses I thought I'd misplaced several days earlier.

Butterflies

Daniel King

Satellites with solar wings
Titanium butterflies that drift
Larva free around the moon
In black and white eclipsing rings
Flee lycaenid Earthlight rays
To hover bright and perilune
Brittle steel antennae primed
To sip on signals from our shift.

Lava tubes are what we gift
Our regolith descents are timed
Days ahead for early noon
At sunrise Sulawesi's K
Greets our climb and how we sing
Our news as bright as rubies strewn
Filter free, for Earth will lift
Its people crowned like rutile kings.

Requiem for a Toy Soldier

Hollie Dugas

I wipe her tiny green body,
preparing to send it down
a small trench to the Animus,
doing it with a glass of tea
and something other than sadness,
her two stiff arms pointing upward
from her unyielding frame, as if
to ask for a keepsake, something
to take to the place without me.
I kiss the small weapon
fixed to her hand and release
her shiny body through the brown
fissure and into another
flimsy world, mother turtle depositing
hatchlings. In death we see
what's inside, the soft uncertainties
rearranging. When I die, I want to
be palatable, eaten up by a lover's
feelings, the world looking down
on my measly form as it follows
a tea-soaked slice of orange
to the space where I'll be planted
in a small spot of earth, an egg
in the sand, heart-sap ripening.

Crab Spider Hoverfly
Scott Brackey
photography
12x15

Rain Rose Leaf
Scott Brackey
photography
15x20

Guerrilla Warfare

Ruth Maus

The cold, hard edges of me
have their own memory of
time when stakes were driven,
blood was let, left to
define those boundaries —
undisturbed straight lines.

A delicate sensibility threatens
now to mutiny—insidious,
serene treachery, lulling
with its soft caresses those
clever, cold, hard edges.

Unthinkable that part of me
should disobey that tyranny
imposed in pain, inscribed in
blood, which promised to keep
out the world.

But world is waiting. Whether
menace or relief, this gentle
side will cause me grief:
some fractured sentimental fool,
too weak to curb emotion,
torn apart, half kind, half cruel.

Occupying the Body

Carol V. Davis

Moving into someone else's house is like occupying the body.
You recognize it as human but the clothes don't quite fit.
The voice leaking from your throat croaks with words
you would never use.

This rust colored kitchen has horizontal windows
slightly larger than the slits in castle walls.
More like the eyebrows of metal filings we'd slash with a magic
wand onto Wooly Willy, that cartoon face from our childhoods.

You can tell this is not earthquake country.
Plates and bowls stack on an open shelf; various-sized glasses
huddle on a wire rack nudging one another;
school children bunched for a class photo.

I wander room to room, feeling for light switches.
Investigating this new body to see if I am just a squatter,
a dybbuk forcing her way in, waiting to fly out when the time is right.

Negative Mass

Sarah Moore Wagner

The lesson said stillness: there was a satellite
orbiting a spot of dust nearby as a moon would,
as I do you. I am trying to be still, want to
learn the darkness, the sky. Night, I want to explore
what it means to hold my palm up and toward you:
Call me something else, not star or a streak of matter,
call me solar heat. I want you
to crank up the energy of the light you leave on for me,
for it to create mass, turn to mass, turn to a bud,
then blossom, then vapor, or a shadow of a vapor
or baby, to curl and leave a track of something re-creatable
in every way, an imperfect image, myself something imperfect here.
Myself and another thing to destroy it or us, as if self image
were an image of creation.

The Mennonite Lady of Pelkie

Peter Hoheisel

Splayed on a wooden porch
her naked feet announce
themselves
because the rest of her
from the cap
on top of her head
to the long, flowing dress
covering her ankles, is hidden.

All around her,
earth vibrates with joy as
the blooming, greening,
billowing of August
springs toward the sky
from the rich brown dirt
of the vegetable patch which she tends.

With roots in heaven,
she is entirely immersed in
earthiness,
cats wandering around,
curious about strangers,
a horse in the field,
and firewood stacked neatly,
awaiting the cold and grey
of November
while her two young girls,
swaddled in tiny, shy dresses,
peek from behind,
her voluminous skirt,
examining the ones who are visiting.

Her bare feet root her
to the land
which blossoms at her touch,
yet she reeks of heaven,
because she knows
that earth is a fragile gift,
a speck of time
in our span of existence,
each day an opportunity
to unlearn
the ego bite of apple
which banishes us from Eden.

The sensuality of her
understated self
makes her shine brighter
than any Hollywood starlet,
affirming, affirming, affirming.

To we
who are rooted
in neither earth nor heaven,
who dance across the surface of things,
bewildered by fear and imaginings,
she is a living chastisement.
We, who spin and tumble
in the endless agonies of ego,
are astonished
in the sensuality of
her brazen, barefoot existence.

A Working-Class Death

Carrie La Seur

Your dad is dying. You've known it for months but the nurse is serious tonight when she calls and asks you to come sit with him in his narrow room at the veterans' home. He's in the later stages of congestive heart failure, complicated by diabetes, obesity, gout, prostate problems and whatever other trouble years of poor diet, little exercise, long work hours and minimal health care will get you. That he held out until age 70 is a little medical miracle and not much credit to the VA, which can't keep track of his records.

You keep track of his records.

He's propped up in pajamas on rough white sheets, working for each breath. You swab his mouth as it hangs open, showing discolored and misplaced teeth he could never afford to fix. His skin is mottled both from age and from the cystic acne that's plagued him all his life. An oxygen tube would help but he's asked for no interventions, no heroics. That's the Dad you remember, the long-suffering Marine who was proud to serve when his number came up. He finished basic at the head of his platoon. Now he takes chronic pain as another heavy pack to carry, mile after mile.

Your brother would like to be here but he's at work on the West Coast and can't afford time off. It's a theme in your family, not having money for things that are important. Your parents divorced 15 years ago when Dad lost his job as a grocery buyer and took one with worse hours, conditions, and pay—managing a convenience store, if you must know—in another state. Enough, your mother said. She'd followed him on a trail of nowhere cities and inadequate employment that would end with taking a stand in a cold, dusty northern plains town you couldn't get out of fast enough.

Your dad barely opens his eyes but reaches out to grasp your hand. Although you're a grown woman and a lawyer with an urgent case file to read at his bedside at midnight, you're still his little girl, the proof that he did something right. He didn't drink like his dad. He didn't hit you more than the occasional spanking. He didn't leave. His greatest parenting accomplishments are acts of omission, but there are also affirmative acts of love. He stopped smoking when you were born. He taught you to ride your bike, drive, fish, salute, hit hard from an unexpected angle and fight back against anyone who looked down on you.

He taught you that people will look down on you—but he didn't mean to. He knows no other way to see the world. You're ashamed to remember the times you've been ashamed of him—for his cheap short sleeve dress shirts, his gut, the way he picks his teeth with his pocket knife and quotes country music lyrics—because he's always been so proud of you. He achieved what no one in his family ever had: he got a college degree. Sure he almost flunked out, pool sharking to make ends meet where the GI Bill didn't quite cover the needs of a family, but he graduated when neither of his parents had finished 8th grade. You suspect that you have no idea how hard that really was.

"How'd you get a woman like her to marry someone like you?" a colleague asked Dad at a work dinner once when Mom wore her one string of fake pearls and a little black dress that made her look like Jackie O. The story hung on in the family for years, a pretty compliment to Mom embedded with the kind of put down Dad absorbed all his life. With his bottle-bottom glasses, bad skin, bad teeth, cheap suit, and shaggy haircut, he makes a terrible first impression, a walking sitcom punch line, and he knows it. He's also funny and a good singer and can be kind if he isn't provoked, but most people wouldn't take the time to know him that well.

It took adulthood to make you wonder how he stumbled so badly when it came to solidifying his place in the middle class. For a while you thought it was his unique failings, an inability to assimilate, and surely appearance and social skills are part of the story. Then you began to look around you in towns like those you grew up in and saw that his appearance is nothing unusual. It's the look of people who have zero disposable income to spend on themselves, especially the men, who wash their hair with a bar of soap, brush their teeth, and rush to work in whatever's clean. It's the outward appearance of poverty.

We make careful visual distinctions in this country. "Dress like the job you want" also means, if you can't dress and groom that way, good luck getting that job. You're your father's daughter, so you know the penalty of looking the wrong way, but you're also uneasy with passing as upper class, no matter what your education and salary. The working class made you and at some fundamental level you're loyal to it. The reflexive mockery of the people you come from by the people around you bites every time. When Hannibal Lecter says to Clarice Starling, "You're just one generation removed from poor white trash"—oh you feel that. You know the gaze the monster turns on her. You've spent years avoiding it.

But in your father's prime working years, the seventies through the nineties, larger forces were amassing against Americans who grew up in poverty believing in the bootstrap American dream. During that period, wages stagnated then shuffled into a decided downward trend. He got minimal raises and tiny bonuses, never grossing over $30,000 a year at his highest salary. There was no pension. He cashed out his IRA to put a down payment on a house after the divorce. Like tens of millions of Americans, you never had dental coverage growing up and learned to brush and floss compulsively while your dad paid for his root canal out of his own pocket.

You have dental insurance now. He never did.

In many ways you're exceptional among not just your family but your generation. You've risen above your origins while others, including family members, have fallen back even from their own highest social standing. The single-wide trailer house you moved your dad out of when his health failed was an anchor and an oracle. It said, "Don't get too high and mighty. You could wind up here too." Yet even as he experienced the sort of setbacks that have turned many white men bitter and angry—and there was bitterness and anger enough—your dad hasn't turned against his class. He's a yellow dog Democrat who's voted and argued all his life for the honor and rights of the working man, the laborer, the veteran against the forces that would crush them.

And now he's dying. You should have done better for him, found other doctors, spent more time, but you were working long hours at the firm. You have a child of your own. You had so little to give, after all he gave you, and that's the way of your family too—never enough to go around. Never enough self-esteem or social capital, never enough sanity or sobriety, never enough love, because even though you were loved, the greeting card trope is true: to love someone else, you have to love yourself first. Your dad loved you as best he could, but his real gift was the sense of inadequacy that drives you.

He won't let go of your hand. He's waited for this night, you realize, when you'd be here and he could die holding his little girl's hand, accompanied into the unknown. He doesn't want to die alone so you have to stay as hours pass, testimony blurs before your eyes, and the hard chair hurts your back and legs. His breaths rasp. If you look up you can follow each one, the inflation of blue-veined, hollowed cheeks, the rise of gown and blanket, parched lips you moisten with a sponge on a lollipop stick.

There's a little gasp and then silence. He's not hooked up to machines so you have to stand over him to be sure that no breath or heartbeat stirs him. His eyes opened at the end, facing death with a brave heart, you imagine. You put your hand on his eyelids like they do in police dramas and shut them. You kiss his cheek and say, "Goodbye Daddy."

You put your head down on his soft, limp hand and cry.

Aquari
Eliot Eckersley
ink and watercolor
5.5x8.5

Flight Lessons

John Sibley Williams

If I could make you a necklace of dead suns
strung together by the light they still give off,
I probably wouldn't. My hands are too dark
a church, my thumbs too fat & clumsy to hold
things that closely. If I could translate, roughly,
your skin on mine, your arms woven through
& back out me, like a knot: a hanging knot:
its loosening, would I bother with the sky,
its cold poetries, this skein of distance?
All the wooden airplanes I've carved for our kids
out of my own vague desires, if I could only
make them fly. If I could learn current & lift,
gravity, what it is that keeps birds from crash,
maybe what dropped would remain aloft, forever,
secure in their own poorly whittled wings.

Scriabin vs. the Birds

Maxima Kahn

The day's a lit branch,
    held out, arm's length, glittering,
inviting us to take it,
    take it in. Silence
filled with muted calls of birds,
    Scriabin filtering through the walls.

So quiet the calls of birds are a delicate *pianissimo*,
        interrupted by the cacophony
of a distant rooster crowing.
        The world so still
there's nothing to add to it.

So i watch and listen,
    when so much saying seems a waste,
when even Scriabin, perfectly tuned
        to this morning mood, sounds like indoor art,
something he was doing when he might better
        be out in this.

Perhaps where he was,
        was grey, a rainy city, little to see
but pavement and grime,
    the hustle bustle.

i give thanks for his creation
    even as it falls short
of this light caressing my skin,
    putting coins of silver in the trees,
falls short of the filigree of this subtler score,
    so exquisite in its detail, so fine.

I'm the Queen of the Rumba Beat

Isabel Gaddis

Right now I like the sound
of Desi Arnaz
singing "Cuban Pete"
more than just about anything else.

Desi sings it for me over and over, from inside my little phone.
"It's very nice, so full of spice."

I cannot get over that line.
It's very clunky, so very awkward.
But José Norman wrote it down
and every time Desi Arnaz sang "Cuban Pete"
(which was a lot of times),
he had to put a little spin on "so full of spice,"
so it would sound sexy.
And he did,
give that flat-footed line a twirl,
around and around.
(To be fair, José was from Liverpool—"Joseph Sternberg," to start—
and Liverpool didn't get sexy till about 50 years after he was born.)

I am a little clunky myself,
but if I had a beautiful singing voice
it would be somebody's job
to make me look
enticing.
To paint pointy stripes of eyeliner along my crinkly eyes;
to make my hair stand up off my scalp;
to get me to stop holding my hands that way;
and to stop making that face.

Chick chicky boom,
chick chicky boom,
chick chicky boom.

The Tectonics of Words

Ken Holland

Of course words break bones—
Consonants like sledgehammers
Letters bricked into syllables

I bring my words to you on a pallet
An industrial forklift lays them at your feet
My voice is carried on waves of diesel fume

If I've asked you to bear more weight
Than I could have borne myself, for what it's worth,
I'm breaking too

The Earth is a fracturing of land masses—
Vaalbara, Laurentia, Rodinia, Avalonia, Gondwana, Pangaea—
We've been breaking apart for four billion years

And we name each of these ruptures
As if to cauterize their broken boundaries

Come
This is my hand I've laid at the ocean's edge
These are my fingers beckoning you

The sun will expire in five billion years
That's all the time we have
To pull ourselves back together.

Another Question

Lois Marie Harrod

after May Swenson

Body my turtle
my spider my crab
what will I do

when carapace
disintegrates
and I no longer pelt?

Where will I crawl,
scuttle and spin—
this skin so sensitive

to thorn and sting.
How to scurry
scamper, dash

without the barn
on my back,
are we not

what we lug
from sea to wen?
I’ve always feared

criticism.
Where will I hunt?
What will I know?

Will there be
any hide left
when hide goes?

In Memory Yet Gold

J. David Liss

Hal was already in the kitchen having a cup of coffee when Ellen entered, wrapped in a white terrycloth bathrobe. She walked into the rectangle of yellow sunlight pouring onto the kitchen floor from the window, and her white robe and pale hair glowed with golden highlights.

He looked at her as if he had been waiting for just this moment. He said, "*The Woman in Gold*. What was the first name of the artist who painted that? I remember his last name was Klimt, but I can't remember his first name."

Her smile at him was as warm as the sun coming through the window. "Gustav."

He smiled back. "And do you remember Klimt's painting, *The Kiss*? There were two people in that painting, but I can't remember what they were doing. Do you think you can show me? For art's sake, of course."

She walked into his arms and kissed him, ignoring his gray stubble. "I don't know who this guy Art is, but I'm happy to help him out."

"Now if I could remember the first guy who used that line, I'd have a perfect memory and be about 5,000 years old."

She went through her mental checklist. He had remembered how to use the Keurig machine. He remembered to put a mug in it before starting it. She had filled the machine's reservoir the night before, so she wasn't worried about it running out of water. He remembered to put the milk back in the refrigerator. Nothing was spilled on the floor. And he was making fun of his own memory loss.

This was going to be a good day.

"What day is it today?" He asked that question every couple of hours. Well, she couldn't blame him. Ever since they retired she had trouble keeping track of the days; they all felt like weekends.

"It's Saturday, and Debra's coming over with Robert." She always said their son-in-law's name, both to remind Hal that his name was Robert and that their daughter was married.

"Well, it's been too long since Debra was here. And I want to catch up on how Robert is doing with his fellowship."

What the heck! Almost correct on two counts. Debra hadn't been there in almost a month. Hal was right, it had been too long since she last visited. She'd had a two-week shift and then went on vacation. Ellen was missing her too. There were times when Hal complained about Debra never visiting the day after she had been there. On the "glass is half full" side of the ledger, at least Hal remembered that Robert was a physician. However, he had finished his neurology fellowship several years ago and was on staff at the hospital.

Then came the coup de grace. "Maybe when Robert finishes his fellowship, he'll figure out a cure for Alzheimer's in time for it to help me."

Four long seconds of silence, then Ellen said, "I see you made coffee for yourself. How 'bout a cup for your old wife?"

"Did I acquire a new wife?"

Their banter felt like the days before the Alzheimer's was in their life and it started to make her feel sad. He was lucid, but it wouldn't last, and he would go back to helplessness and confusion and needing to be guided through every part of his day. She hoped he could last for this whole day so that Debra and Robert could enjoy "the real" Hal.

"Hal, we have time for one cup of coffee each. Deb and Rob are coming for breakfast and they're bringing the bagels. We have about 45 minutes to have one cup and get dressed and get the house ready."

"Do we have eggs in the house? I'll make scrambled eggs. The kids love my scrambled eggs. Harry says that he'll win his wife the way I won you; I made scrambled eggs that were so good that you wanted to spend the night with me so that I would make you breakfast."

"You told Harry that I would spend the night with you in order to get scrambled eggs?" Harry was their son, gone these 10 years from the cancer that killed him.

"Absolutely not! I was simply answering the question he asked: why was mom willing to marry you to begin with? And he extrapolated from that." This was like the old Hal— so precise with his language.

"I think Debbie and Rob are bringing smoked fish, so we probably won't be having eggs."

"Are you kidding? We'll have both. Debra loves my eggs as much as Harry. I've told them the secret to making the best scrambled eggs in the world; you have to burn the butter before putting the eggs in." Hal used to make delicious eggs by first burning the butter. Of course, lately he burned everything because when he started any recipe, he soon forgot what he was doing and left the kitchen with the burner on. She had been able to discourage him from cooking and did not want him to get back into the habit of using the stove or oven. She lived in fear of immolation or asphyxiation.

"Let's see how hungry everyone is," she answered. As soon as she made that statement, she knew what he was going to say next and silently counted 3, 2, 1.

"Harry is always hungry. I don't know how he stays so skinny."

"Harry won't be joining us today."

"That's too bad. Does he know his sister is coming over?"

"I think so."

"I'll ask Debra and…" Hal paused and Ellen filled in, "Robert."

"That's right, Robert. I'll ask Robert if he wants eggs."

Ellen picked out Hal's clothes and he didn't need any help putting them on. She quickly got herself ready and was able to do a more careful job with her makeup than she'd been doing lately. This was a really good day. She hoped it would last.

The kids arrived with fresh, warm bagels and smoked fish and cream cheese. Debra said, "We've been smelling these bagels for the last 15 minutes; the car smells like a bakery. It's made me ravenous."

Robert added, "At one point, I thought she was going to eat me."

Then Hal said, "It would be hard to spread cream cheese on you." And everyone laughed and Debra and Robert visibly relaxed. Ellen hadn't realized how tense they looked when they walked in, their shoulders hunched forward and flat expressions on their faces. She felt her own shoulders relaxing. Hal was Hal for a while and everyone was at ease.

The kids started cutting bagels and asking Debra's parents what type they wanted, egg, cinnamon raisin, poppy, and so on. They'd brought a dozen bagels just for the four of them, but Debra knew her mother would freeze whatever was left over to have another day. Ellen would say to Debra, "Take these bagels home. You can freeze them and they're delicious toasted." And Debra would answer, "By the time we get home they'll have started to harden. You freeze them. Dad loves bagels." And Ellen would keep them because anything she did not have to do, any store she did not have to go to, any break at all that she could get was really, really needed. Taking care of Hal was a 24/7 job.

Hal then offered his second surprise of the morning. "Who wants scrambled eggs?"

Debra loved her father's scrambled eggs, had for as long as she could remember. Of course, those eggs had gotten a lot of hype throughout her childhood. Mom was the main cook and did the fancy stuff, but Dad made great eggs.

She knew why they were so delicious. He added freshly ground pepper and a little bit of kosher salt, but mostly it was because he burned the butter before adding the eggs. But she had learned that from her late brother Harry. Hal had taught it to him, not her. The way he put it was, "Deb, Harry needs to learn how to make the world's best scrambled eggs so that one day he can attract a wife. I've learned that the one thing that women find irresistible is delicious eggs. This is a secret that can only be passed down through the male heirs of the line. My brothers and I learned it from our father, who learned it from his father. It's the only thing I believe should have a male bias. Scrambled eggs is where I draw the line on egalitarianism."

Of course, as soon as Harry learned it he told Debra. They shared everything. They were very close.

Debra looked at her mother for a clue. Should she let her father cook? She'd heard from her mom that dad almost set the house on fire.

Ellen shrugged. "Hal, I'll have some of those delicious eggs, too."

"Great. How about you, Deb? And you..." (Ellen and Debra held their breath) "Robert?" While Robert would never be insulted if Hal forgot his name, the ladies still felt relieved.

Robert answered, "Not only will I have some of those eggs, but I'll stand with you and watch you make them so that I can pick up the skill." Ellen was grateful that Robert had thought of a way to supervise Hal without insulting him.

Hal began breaking eggs into a bowl, ten of them. The yolks floated like ten days of sunrise. And Hal's face seemed to glow with an inner light, as if inside his head was a planet that had 10 suns that shone down all the time—a sky full of suns.

He reached into the cabinet under the stove and found a 14-inch cast aluminum pan and cut a quarter of a stick of butter into the pan. He turned on the heat, looked in the pan as the butter melted, and added another quarter.

Debra watched him beat the eggs with a fork. It brought her right back to her childhood. The yolks broke and merged under Hal's surprisingly steady hand. As Debra watched the yolks spread and the mixture turn a bright yellow, she thought back 15 years to a speech that her father had made in their Temple.

They went to Temple every Friday night. That was her mom's doing. Ellen really was in charge of the family's spirit. But her father was on the Temple board. He was also on its Capital Campaign Committee, and that night the chair of the committee was going to make a speech announcing the start of the campaign. Her father wanted to be there to support the chairman.

To ensure there would be a large audience in the Temple, and so increase excitement about the campaign, the Rabbi had scheduled an extraordinary musical program that week, and several hundred congregants were present. When they arrived, the committee members retired to a small conference room to wait for the chairman.

The start of services was getting closer and he still wasn't there when the Cantor came into the room. "We just heard from Millie Epstein. Sol slipped on the way out of the house and sprained his back. He'll be fine, but right now he has to lie down flat and he can't move around. He won't be here to make the speech."

As a person, the committee members turned to Hal. The Cantor said, "Hal, can you fill in?" Hal knew how to talk.

"Sure. Let me go into the office and jot down some notes."

About an hour later he gave the speech. Debra didn't remember all of it, but she remembered the opening and the main images.

"I'm guessing that most of you didn't wake at dawn to see the sun rise. But you sure enough expected the sun to be in the sky to light your day. That's a reasonable expectation. Whether you're a Rabbi or a physicist…" (here he looked behind himself and nodded to their Rabbi, who was indeed a physicist in addition to being clergy. The congregants got the joke) "…you may have a different explanation for why the sun rises. But you are very sensible to expect it to be there in the east, shining and golden, heading west as it lights your day.

"The sun lights your day for good or ill, but you have to decide how special you will make this day, each day. You decide where you will shine your light. That's what I'm going to speak with you about today."

Her father had spoken about the golden day that would dawn at their Temple if all the congregants were part of a giving community. At one point he said, "I look at you and see all the cares of your week on your faces. But this is the Sabbath. This is a day of the heart. This is a night for us to smile." And he smiled.

When he smiled, every congregant she saw started smiling. *How does he do that?* she remembered wondering to herself.

He was quite compelling. He made the case, and people responded with a level of generosity that nobody expected.

Debra had always been impressed that her father had made such a good speech with almost no preparation. The talk had been infused with images of the sun and golden light. She had literally felt physically warmed by his words and suspected that the people who gave so generously also felt it.

She was slipping into sadness as she thought about how Alzheimer's had affected her dad, and disrupted the feeling by asking her mother, "Mom, what dish do you want me to put the fish in?"

"Use two dinner platters, one for the nova and one for the baked salmon and the whitefish."

Robert was standing close to Hal, learning how to make the eggs but more to supervise him. The butter in the pan had burned from yellow to dark brown, almost black. Ellen had seen Hal make scrambled eggs for years and knew that when he poured the eggs into the hot pan, they would cook really quickly.

As the eggs swirled into the pan they mixed with the brown-black butter like sunlight mixing with shadows, like when the sun sets in winter. She thought about a train trip they had made one December to the Delaware Art Museum. They decided to take Amtrak to Wilmington instead of driving. It was the first of many train rides they would take to see museums across the East Coast. Hal was on the glide path to retirement and the trip was a first foray into how they planned to structure their lives when he no longer had to work every day. She had discovered the painter John Sloane when she was researching American Impressionists. The little Delaware Museum had the nation's best Sloane collection and they were both excited.

The museum did not disappoint, either, with its collection or how it organized its exhibitions. They returned home at about 4 p.m., with the winter sun setting behind them. As the train rushed north and east, the sun shone through the bare trees, casting shadows and yellow light in front of their path, covering the ground with what to her looked like an abstract painting. In her head, she named the painting *Trees at Dusk*.

Now, in her kitchen years later, she thought of him sitting next to her on the train, occasionally leaning over to kiss her cheek, really so that he could smell her hair. These were hard thoughts, so she looked at Hal and Robert and said, "How are those eggs coming?"

Hal answered. "The pan is coming off the burner right now," and he lifted up the pan and scooped the eggs into a platter that Debra had placed on the counter next to the stove.

Debra, Robert, and Ellen finished getting breakfast on the table, and for a little bit there was silence as they put cream cheese and butter on bagels, layered on smoked fish, and spooned scrambled eggs onto their plates. Robert broke the silence. "These eggs are delicious! Who knew that plain old scrambled eggs could taste this good?"

Hal looked up and said, "You're right. These are delicious. Who made them?"

They were silent. They looked down at their plates. It had seemed like it was going to be a really good day. But the Alzheimer's was reasserting itself.

Hal continued talking. "Whoever the cook is, he must be a genius. These are works of art! So delicious, so perfect. I bet the cook is really handsome too. And virile—now that's a word you don't here too often nowadays. But I'm sensing that the guy who made these eggs is really virile. Ellen, what do you think? Taste these eggs and tell me that you don't think the guy who cooked them must be virile."

Ellen let out a guffaw, more from a sense of relief than humor. She smacked Hal's arm. "You idiot. Stop blowing your own horn and eat the eggs while they're hot."

Hal put down his fork. "A delicious plate of scrambled eggs is like a work of art. It can take a tough day and make it better. It can make you smile." As he said that, he smiled. Ellen and Debra and Robert suddenly found themselves smiling too, they couldn't help it.

Seriously

Les Bernstein

today I lost Gertrude Stein
she was gone for nearly 8 hours and 39 minutes
I remembered her thick ankles
the autobiography she wrote for Alice B.
and of course I did remember
Alice and her cookies
also I recalled how mean
thick ankled Gertrude was
to Hemingway's wife
hell… to all the wives
when she returned
in the Whole Foods parking lot
I could not keep
from screaming her name
and in general
being peeved with her
and her whole deal
a rose is a ...
seriously?

Felinoid Fall
Tanya Shatseva
acrylic on canvas
32x39

Black Hole In The Milky Way
Tanya Shatseva
acrylic on canvas
12x12

Still Life: Mother with Child and Dog in Car

Kelly R. Samuels

Those long drives west to where trees were planted with purpose. Where rocks
were picked from the fields. Heaved into the flatbed. Ground down.

To where she called home. Spoke of fondly. Said we must always go in the spring
and in the summer and in the winter, even if snow. Even if ice.

Leaving early so that sun didn't blind. So that the packed lunch would stay cool
and fresh. The hardboiled eggs peeled, smooth and slick in the hand.

Just two stops to stretch. To refill. To walk to the station door with the key.

This giving over to a dog's whine and cry for the front seat. Paws perched
on the dashboard. All the road ahead within gaze.

But a blanket, she says. And some books, she says. Left unread for the sway and rumble of it, landscape streaming. The stomach's lurch and plummet.

Turning her head sometimes to ask what of. Ask to rummage in her purse for a tissue, for a mint. To extract this or that, handing it over.

Across a wide state, from one border to another. This trinity.

The Center of It All

Ruth Maus

after Ben Lerner

The invalid mother is a big responsibility. And I am the lone guardian. This does not explain my neurosis, however, as I was a mess already. Who am I kidding? I am Mother Teresa, a surefire candidate down the compassionate path of sainthood and hell, I'm not even Catholic. I am some kind of artist,

or I teach tricks to housecats who would otherwise behave like turnips. Sometimes I'm a cleaner of polypropylene carpets, knowing what products take out what stains. Maybe—just saying—I repackage the products in little plastic bottles that I purchase at the dollar store and give them away at dirty bus stops to dirty people. My guilty pleasure would be redesigning the human body for maximum efficiency, a Volvo's engineering, all redemptive and able to withstand

violence. We all die sometime. Maybe I am somebody who measures capacity. I could throw down the gauntlet to those terrorists who confiscate it. I'm already a terrorist myself at the center of it all. I know this because I take charge in a crisis and because the numbers don't lie. How many times have you been in the

hospital? But I am not who you think I am. I appear calm when the hospice folks call to tell me of a new wound or the need for pureed everything. I smile when dealing with doctors and nurses and appointments and meds and special compounded meds not covered by insurance. I purchase the lift, the incontinence products, the wheelchair, all approved with my excellent credit history. The expense like a chisel, like groaning. Maybe I absorb the fat shitstorm of nursing homes and Medicare. Even when I can never take a vacation or a day off, life flattens like a midway of nice manners. I have encountered a theory of unborn innocence. Actually I made it up, what with the lack of innocence and I'm pretty well born at this point. Maybe even old. It goes like this: why can we all help each other during a crisis, but after the soup and after the protoplasm and after the rosary, when the other drivers get behind the wheel everyone becomes rude? Honk if you are rude.

The Abacist

Denton Loving

I remember that man well
who sat with an abacus, unendingly
patient—one of those men
who counted tobacco sheaths,
casks of wine and rice paddies
as easily as he tallied
quantities of grain in the shadows
of the great pyramids—
his fine, nimble fingers
sliding stones over a board of sand.

No one knew the truth of his past.
He had been born on an island.
He watched the ibis
wade the marsh for crustaceans.
He believed the ibis
gifted man with mathematics,
the moon and magic.
So he counted the birds like
seers count crows, computing
meaning beyond their numbers.

On clear nights, he counted stars
until his eyelids grew too heavy
to stay awake. In dreams,
he counted lost loves, their nights
together and nights apart
growing like twin-row crops
in the same acre of ache.

Conventional wisdom says
we count to remember
the details of our existence.
The abacist knew
we often count to forget—
all these numbers mere
calculations against loneliness.

Desensitized

Marc Meierkort

for Mike Thurn (1970–1986)

These poems.
I can't stand to look at 'em anymore.
These misshapen words. These haphazard impulses to direct
emotion into syntax & structure. I erase all the old attempts,
only really sure of a title, & your name.

Erasure is easy as a button, a scissor-shaped icon where I cut
your memory up into dated bookends & weight.
I cannot go back to retrieve these pieces of remembrance
hatched into keystrokes, embalmed in silicon.
I talk to you now directly.

I dream you are dead. Still, I know it. Ask you about it.
You don't answer. Just mouth some words swept away
with the wind, throw something towards me, telling
your stories about a guy named Seymour & his irreverent bottles
of distilled water. No one else seems to remember these stories.

The song they play by your grave doesn't get played at parties anymore.
There are no parties like that anymore. I hope you don't mind
me talking to you now instead of writing about you.
Ever use just the right colors, but still stumble outside the lines?
Ever feel more like stained glass among the ivy trails of ales & wines?

You are my prisoner:
my impulse to fulfill the notion of loss, my regard for tragedy,
my return to dark humor, my impulse to fulfill a requirement for elegy,
my regard for irony, my return to cinematic outcomes,
my impulse to fulfill the need to grieve.

You are not an experience anymore.

You are a not-very-good-poem that hounds me
like a failing grade. I shed that excuse, give you back your true poetics.
Thanks for that visit while I slept, wrestling with the remote,
control not something I'm bound to obey, making me give
you back your name. No one wants to be the epigrammatic blind quote.
I almost forget how to miss you when you are gone.
You are facing me every time I open this file, & that title & your name
throttle me into deleting the words of your memory.
Words shouldn't be for you but from you: your voice, your stories,
your irreverent invasions of dream saved as something more than an anecdote
or poem. I cannot stand to see you like this. You cannot breathe underneath
my tendency to overstate. I'm tired of writing about you & visiting you only
among toolbars & cursors. I'd rather hear about Seymour in dream.
I'm done with you.

CONTRIBUTORS

Glen Armstrong holds an M.F.A. in English from the University of Massachusetts, Amherst and teaches writing at Oakland University in Rochester, Michigan. He edits the poetry journal *Cruel Garters*, and his work has appeared in *Poetry Northwest, Conduit,* and *Cloudbank.*

Les Bernstein lives in Mill Valley, Calif. Her chapbooks, *Borderland, Naked Little Creatures*, and *Amid the Din*, have been published by Finishing Line Press (2011, 2012, 2015). She has won the Nazim Hikmet Award for 2015 and was a Pushcart Prize nominee for 2016.

Scott Brackey is a 2015 graduate of Washburn University with a degree in history and currently serves the community at the Topeka & Shawnee County Public Library. A self-taught hobbyist, he enjoys exploring nature through the unique perspectives of macro and landscape photography.

Sarah Brown Weitzman, a past National Endowment for the Arts fellow in poetry, is widely published in journals and anthologies including *New Ohio Review, North American Review, Bellingham Review, Rattle, Mid-American Review, Poet Lore, Miramar, Spillway*, and elsewhere. Her books are available from Amazon.

Susana H. Case is the author of four chapbooks and six books of poetry, most recently *Erasure, Syria* from Recto y Verso Editions (2018). Her first collection, *The Scottish Café,* from Slapering Hol Press (2002), was re-released in a dual-language English-Polish version, *Kawiarnia Szkocka,* by Opole University Press in Poland.

Sandy Coomer, an artist and poet, is the author of three poetry chapbooks. Her art has been featured in local shows and exhibitions and has appeared in literary art journals such as *Lunch Ticket, Varnish*, and *Inklette*, among others. She lives in Brentwood, Tenn.

Carol V. Davis is the author of *Because I Cannot Leave This Body* (Truman State University Press, 2017), *Between Storms* (TSUP, 2012), and *Into the Arms of Pushkin: Poems of St. Petersburg* (TSUP, 2007), for which she received the T.S. Eliot Prize. She teaches at Santa Monica College and Antioch University, Los Angeles.

Hollie Dugas lives and teaches in New Mexico. Her work appears in *Barrow Street, Fugue, Phoebe, Pembroke, Potomac Review, Under the Gum Tree, Folio, Slipstream, Jelly Bucket, The Tulane Review*, and *CALYX*. Her poem "A Woman's Confession #5,162" was recently selected as the winner of *Western Humanities Review* Mountain West Writers' Contest. She is a member on the editorial board for *Off the Coast*.

Eliot Eckersley is a junior at Washburn University majoring in film and minoring in anthropology. She enjoys participating in art challenge months and "draw this in your own style" challenges. When she's not busy with school or art, she enjoys watching Netflix and making Vine jokes with her roommate.

Andrew Foster is a philosophy major and English minor from central Kansas. His self-taught painting style combines street art/graffiti performance and technique with Bob Ross's iconic "wet on wet" painting method in an attempt to foster a "try this at home" atmosphere around art and its creation.

Isabel Gaddis earned her bachelor's degree in earth and planetary sciences from M.I.T. and worked as a geophysicist at Shell, then as a technical writer and copywriter at Microsoft. She studied playwriting at Freehold Theatre in Seattle, writing for television at UCLA, screenwriting with Corey Mandell, and creative writing with Jack Grapes.

Jack Granath is a librarian in Kansas. His poetry has appeared in *Poetry East, Rattle*, and *North American Review*, among other journals and magazines.

Carrie Greenlaw is a poet and artist from the north side of Pittsburgh. Her work has been published in *The Pittsburgh Poetry Review*, and she has appeared as a featured reader for *The New Yinzer Presents.*

Ira Joel Haber was born and lives in Brooklyn. He is a sculptor, painter, writer, book dealer, photographer, and teacher. His work has appeared in group shows in both the U.S. and Europe and he has had nine one-man shows including several retrospectives of his sculpture. His work is in the collections of The Whitney Museum of American Art, New York University, The Guggenheim Museum, The Hirshhorn Museum, The Albright-Knox Art Gallery and The Allen Memorial Art Museum.

Benjamin Harnett is a historian, fiction writer, poet, and digital engineer. His works have appeared recently in *Pithead Chapel, Brooklyn Quarterly, Moon City Review*, and *Tahoma Literary Review*. His story "Delivery" was chosen as *Longform's* "Story of the Week." He holds an M.A. in classics from Columbia University, and in 2005 co-founded the fashion brand Hayden-Harnett. He lives in Beacon, N.Y., with his wife, Toni, and their pets. He can be found most days on Twitter, @ benharnett. He works for *The New York Times.*

Lois Marie Harrod's 16th and most recent collection, *Nightmares of the Minor Poet*, appeared in 2016 from Five Oaks. She is continually published in literary journals and online ezines from *American Poetry Review* to *Zone 3*. Visit her online work at www.loismarieharrod.org.

Peter Hoheisel taught creative writing, literature, and composition at Lon Morris College in Jacksonville, Texas, and served as the chair of the Department of Religion and Philosophy there. Earlier, he was awarded numerous grants to teach poetry in schools through the Michigan Council for the Arts and in Tyler, Texas, under a grant from the Texas Commission for the Arts.

Ken Holland has had poetry published in several dozen literary journals, including *Confrontation, Rattle, The Cortland Review*, and *The Antigonish Review*. His work has been nominated for a Pushcart Prize and has won, or placed in, a number of contests. He's just completed his first chapbook collection. He pulls a paycheck working for a New York publisher.

Louisa Howerow's poems appear in recent issues of *Red Earth Review, Nimrod International,* and *Queen's Quarterly*. Her poetry has also been included in anthologies, most recently *Imaginarium 4: The Best Canadian Speculative Writing* (ChiZine Publications, 2015) and *River of Earth and Sky: Poems for the Twenty-First Century* (Blue Light Press, 2015).

Maxima Kahn teaches writing and creative process and blogs about creative, soulful living at BrilliantPlayground.com. Her poetry has appeared in *Sweet, Meridian Anthology of Contemporary Poetry, Tule Review, Poem, Borderlands: Texas Poetry Review, Eureka Literary Magazine,* and elsewhere. She has twice been nominated for Best of the Net.

AKaiser-Veyrat is a member of the poetry collective Sweet Action and contributor to its four chapbooks. You can also read her work in *Amsterdam Quarterly, Crosswinds Poetry Journal, Manzano Mountain Review,* and elsewhere. Her poem "The Sound of Clothes" was the *Sow's Ear Poetry Review* 2017 poetry prize winner. She is also currently working on a biography of urbanista Cebrià Montoliu, the first Iberian translator of Whitman's *Leaves of Grass* into Catalan.

Daniel King is an Australian writer. His poetry collection, *Amethysts and Emeralds*, was published by Interactive Press in May (2018).

Carrie La Seur's debut novel, *The Home Place* (William Morrow, 2014), won the High Plains Book Award and was short-listed for the Strand Critics Award for Best First Novel. La Seur released *The Weight of An Infinite Sky* (William Morrow) in 2018. Her writing appears in *The Daily Beast, The Guardian, Harvard Law & Policy Review, The Kenyon Review Online, The Rumpus,* and *Salon.*

Yue Li was born in Sichuan Province, China, in 1998. The colors in her artwork become the language to express her personal emotions and feelings. She is currently an art student at Washburn University, working towards her B.F.A. in drawing and painting.

J. David Liss earned an M.F.A. from Brooklyn College in 1984. Trained in writing, inclined to politics, he became a speechwriter. His prose has been published in *Inwood Indiana Press, The MacGuffin, Lake Effect, Adelaide*, and others. He has poetry in *Fifth Wednesday Journal, Blood and Thunder, Euphony*, and others.

Denton Loving is the author of the poetry collection *Crimes Against Birds* (Main Street Rag, 2014) and editor of *Seeking Its Own Level*, an anthology of writings about water (MotesBooks, 2014). His writing has recently appeared in *River Styx, CutBank, The Kenyon Review,* and *The Chattahoochee Review*. Follow him on Twitter, @DentonLoving.

Ruth Maus has followed a love of learning around the world and arrived back home in Topeka, Kansas. She represented Smith College at the annual Glasscock Intercollegiate Poetry Contest. Her poems have appeared in *Grecourt Review* and *Lighten Up Online*, and her book of poetry, *Valentine*, will published by Meadowlark Press in 2019.

Marc Meierkort had three poems published about 25 years ago. The journals no longer exist. A lifelong Chicago resident, he has taught English at Thornton Fractional North High School in Calumet City, Ill., for the past 19 years. He is a graduate of Southern Illinois University at Carbondale (B.S.) and National-Louis University (M.A.T.).

Teresa Milbrodt is the author of two short-story collections, *Bearded Women: Stories* (Chizine Publications, 2011) and *Work Opportunities: Stories* (Portage Press, 2018); a novel, *The Patron Saint of Unattractive People* (Boxfire Press, 2013); and a flash fiction collection, *Larissa Takes Flight: Stories* (Booth Books, 2014).

Sara Moore Wagner is the Cincinnati-based author of the chapbook *Hooked Through* (Five Oaks Press, 2017). Her poetry has appeared in many journals and anthologies including *Glass, Gulf Stream, Gigantic Sequins, Stirring,* and *Arsenic Lobster*, among others, and is forthcoming in journals such as *Western Humanities Review* and *Cider Press Review*. She spends her days caring for her three small children, Cohen, Daisy, and Vivienne. Find her at www.saramoorewagner.com.

Katy Mullins's work has appeared or is forthcoming in *Bayou Magazine, South Dakota Review,* and *Litro*, among others. She received her bachelor's in English writing from the University of Pittsburgh. She currently lives in Tulsa, Oklahoma, where she is on the editorial board of *Nimrod International Journal* and teaches high school.

JoDean Nicolette is a physician and teacher who has dedicated herself to a career in writing. JoDean's work has appeared in such publications as *The Sun Magazine, Printers Row Journal,* and *Sugared Water*, and she was awarded the grand prize for prose in *The Maine Review's* Rocky Coast Contest. She lives in western Montana with her dogs and horses, and her extremely patient husband, Ben.

Laurie Reiche lives part-time in London, where she concentrates on photographing the city, particularly Virginia Woolf's Bloomsbury. She has won first place in several contests, including the Riverrun Literary Publication of the University of Colorado Poetry Competition, the national Charlotte Newberger Poetry Prize, and the Mendocino Coast Writers' Conference Contest.

Kelly R. Samuels lives in the upper Midwest. Her poetry has been nominated for Best of the Net and has appeared or is forthcoming in numerous journals, including *The Carolina Quarterly, Sweet Tree Review, Salt Hill, Permafrost,* and *RHINO*. Her chapbook, *Words Some of Us Rarely Use*, was published this year by Unsolicited Press.

Tanya Shatseva is a traditional artist based in Saint Petersburg, Russia. She creates acrylic paintings and illustrations in the genre of pop surrealism. The majority of her works depict subjects in metaphysical scenes and states of twisted perception. They appear in various galleries and are held in private collections around the world.

John Sibley Williams is the author of *As One Fire Consumes Another* (2018 Orison Poetry Prize, Orison Books, 2019) and *Skin Memory* (2018 Backwaters Prize, Backwaters Press, 2019). An eleven-time Pushcart nominee and winner of various awards, John serves as editor of *Inflectionist Review*. Publications include *The Yale Review, Atlanta Review, Prairie Schooner, The Massachusetts Review,* and *Third Coast.*

Kody Stadler is a writer and photographer presently living in Topeka, Kansas. His writing has previously appeared in *Quail Bell Magazine*, and his photographs have been displayed in the Mulvane Art Museum, Two Wolves Studio, and coffee shops nearby. For inquiries/hate mail, please email kody.stadler@gmail.com.

James Sullivan has split his adult life between the American Midwest and central Japan. His work has appeared in *Blotterature* and *The Intentional.* Currently he writes and teaches in Mankato, Minn., while completing an M.F.A.

Larry Thacker's poetry is in over 150 publications including *Spillway, Still: The Journal, Valparaiso Poetry Review, The American Journal of Poetry, Poetry South,* and *Appalachian Heritage*. His publications include the *Drifting in Awe* (Finishing Line Press, 2017) and the forthcoming collections *Feasts of Evasion* (Future Cycle Press, 2019) and *Grave Robber Confessional* (Main Street Rag, 2019).

Charly Verger is an artist who uses painting and writing to express her feelings and her vision of the world (and sometimes of the other world...). Each painting is like a book that you just have to open to read the story which is between the lines.

www.ingramcontent.com/pod-product-compliance
Lightning Source LLC
Chambersburg PA
CBHW061105100726
47911CB00012B/405
9781732183902